91

—— The Coastal Cruising Handbook ——

# ——The Coastal Cruising Handbook——

**Joseph Harand**

Translated from the French by
**Frank George**
Deputy Editor, The Journal of Navigation

**HOLLIS & CARTER**
LONDON   SYDNEY   TORONTO

British Library Cataloguing
in Publication Data
Harand, Joseph
   The coastal cruising handbook.
   1. Yachts and yachting – Europe
   I. Title
   797.1'24      GV817.E85

ISBN 0 370 30220 6
Originally published in France by the author as *Le Mousse*
© J. Harand 1976, 1977
© J. Harand and Librairie Arthaud 1978
British edition © The Bodley Head 1980
Printed in Great Britain for
Hollis & Carter
an associate company of
The Bodley Head Ltd
9 Bow Street, London WC2E 7AL
by Redwood Burn Ltd,
Trowbridge & Esher
Design and Phototypesetting by
Parkway Group, London and Abingdon
*First published in Great Britain 1980*

# ——Author's Foreword——

Coastal cruising is the most popular and enjoyable form of sailing – and the one most fraught with hazards unless undertaken with a certain degree of method.

This little book is devised to help the coastwise yachtsman by putting at his finger-tips all relevant information in a form most quickly assimilated: in visual terms, with a minimum of words. The book is carefully planned and the reader is recommended to read it through closely instead of skimming the pages.

Each page or double-page opening answers the given question in a few seconds.

There are some 500 clear diagrams in place of chapters that might run to several pages.

The pages at the end, lettered instead of numbered, give theoretical context; it is recommended to read these pages first for a clearer understanding of the solution to the practical problems.

The book has been devised methodically and gives best results if studied methodically over a number of sessions.

For the English-speaking reader the translator has included some new material on the Buoyage System and the Collision Regulations. The useful outline of weather forecasts for Continental and Mediterranean waters has been retained, but the tidal sections have been adapted for use with the *Admiralty Tide Tables* or those to be found in such almanacs as the venerable *Reed's* which the English-speaking yachtsman is more likely to have at hand.

No prior knowledge of the theory or practice of navigation is required of the reader and, step by step, the book will take him through the incidents and manoeuvres of his voyage, from knowing his craft, the water he sails and the marks by which he shapes his course, to the remoter contingencies of grounding and shipwreck.

The book is intended for beginners who have at least made a trip in a dinghy. It is also a quick reference work for yacht skippers.

In the hope that it will be found useful, and remembering always that in sailing there are no hard and fast rules – you must welcome hard work, time for reflection, and the challenge of the unforeseen – we wish you a prosperous voyage.

J. H.

# Contents

**Return to harbour**

**Appendices**

# ──Weather Forecasts──

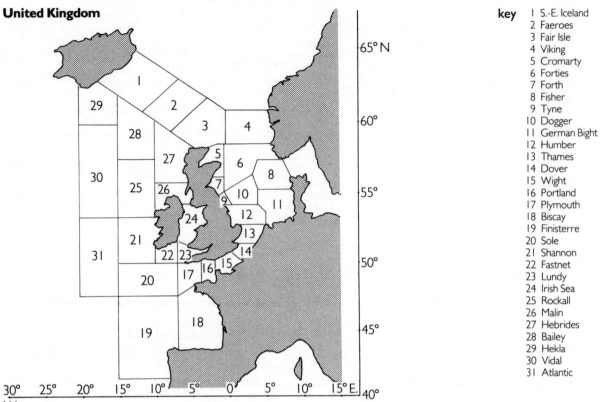

**United Kingdom**

key
1 S.-E. Iceland
2 Faeroes
3 Fair Isle
4 Viking
5 Cromarty
6 Forties
7 Forth
8 Fisher
9 Tyne
10 Dogger
11 German Bight
12 Humber
13 Thames
14 Dover
15 Wight
16 Portland
17 Plymouth
18 Biscay
19 Finisterre
20 Sole
21 Shannon
22 Fastnet
23 Lundy
24 Irish Sea
25 Rockall
26 Malin
27 Hebrides
28 Bailey
29 Hekla
30 Vidal
31 Atlantic

|  | Civil Time | Stations | Frequencies | | Zones | Observations |
|---|---|---|---|---|---|---|
|  |  |  | kHz | metres |  |  |
| Times liable to modification | 0015 | BBC Radio 2 | 200 | 1500 | 1–31 |  |
|  | 0625 | BBC Radio 2 | 200 | 1500 | 1–31 |  |
|  | 0655 | BBC Radio 3 | 1215 | 247 | Inshore | 0755 Sat, Sun |
|  | 0745 | Jersey | 1726 | 173.8 | 16 |  |
|  | 0903 | North Foreland | 1848 | 162.3 | 13–15 |  |
|  | group A | Humber | 1861 | 161.2 | 11–12 |  |
|  |  | Port Patrick | 1883 | 159.3 | 23–24 |  |
|  | 0933 | Niton | 1834 | 163.5 | 15–16 |  |
|  | group B | Valentia | 1827 | 164.2 | 21–22 |  |
|  |  | Ilfracombe | 2670 | 112.3 | 22–23 |  |
|  | 1345 | Jersey | 1726 | 173.8 | 16 |  |
|  | 1355 | BBC Radio 2 | 200 | 1500 | 1–31 |  |
|  | 1750 | BBC Radio 2 | 200 | 1500 | 1–31 |  |
|  | 1945 | Jersey | 1726 | 173.8 | 16 |  |
|  | 2103 | Group A | — | — | See 0903 |  |
|  | 2133 | Group B | — | — | See 0933 |  |
|  | 2345 | Jersey | 1726 | 173.8 | 16 |  |

# Weather Forecasts

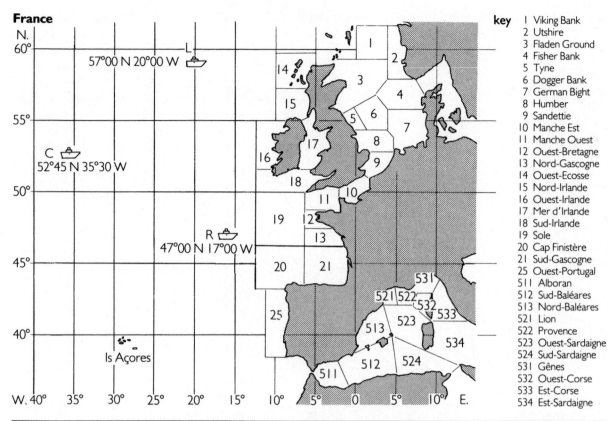

**France**

key

| | |
|---|---|
| 1 | Viking Bank |
| 2 | Utshire |
| 3 | Fladen Ground |
| 4 | Fisher Bank |
| 5 | Tyne |
| 6 | Dogger Bank |
| 7 | German Bight |
| 8 | Humber |
| 9 | Sandettie |
| 10 | Manche Est |
| 11 | Manche Ouest |
| 12 | Ouest-Bretagne |
| 13 | Nord-Gascogne |
| 14 | Ouest-Ecosse |
| 15 | Nord-Irlande |
| 16 | Ouest-Irlande |
| 17 | Mer d'Irlande |
| 18 | Sud-Irlande |
| 19 | Sole |
| 20 | Cap Finistère |
| 21 | Sud-Gascogne |
| 25 | Ouest-Portugal |
| 511 | Alboran |
| 512 | Sud-Baléares |
| 513 | Nord-Baléares |
| 521 | Lion |
| 522 | Provence |
| 523 | Ouest-Sardaigne |
| 524 | Sud-Sardaigne |
| 531 | Gênes |
| 532 | Ouest-Corse |
| 533 | Est-Corse |
| 534 | Est-Sardaigne |

Labels on map: C 52°45 N 35°30 W, L 57°00 N 20°00 W, R 47°00 N 17°00 W, Is Açores

| Stations | kHz | Metres | Zones | Civil Time | Observations |
|---|---|---|---|---|---|
| §Boulogne | 1694 | 177 | 1–11 | 0803, 1833 | §Gale warnings |
| §Le Conquet | 1673 | 179 | 11–19 | 0700, 0833, 1733, 2253 | 03 and 33 past hour |
| Quimperlé | 1876 | 159 | 11–19, 25 | 0700, 0833, 1733, 2253 | |
| §Saint-Nazaire | 1722 | 173 | 11–21 | 1003, 1903 | * Sat, Sun 0715 |
| §Bordeaux-Arcachon | 1820 | 164 | 20–21 | 0803, 1803 | |
| France-Inter | 164 | 1829 | 9–13, 18–21, 25 | 0850, 1950 | †Sat, Sun 1230 |
| Lille | 1376 | 218 | 10 | 0618*, 0718, 1210†, 1830‡ | |
| Paris | 1070 | 280 | 10 | 0618*, 0718, 1210†, 1830‡ | ‡Sat, Sun 1803 |
| Rennes | 710 | 423 | 11–13 | 0618*, 0718, 1210†, 1830‡ | |
| Brest | 1403 | 214 | 11–13 | 0618*, 0718, 1210†, 1830‡ | |
| Bordeaux | 1205 | 249 | 13, 21 | 0618*, 0718, 1210†, 1830‡ | |
| Limoges | 791 | 379 | 13, 21 | 0618*, 0718, 1210†, 1830‡ | |
| Cross a Etel | 2677 | 112 | 12–13 | 1410 | |
| Cross Med | 2677 | 112 | 521–2 | 0840 | |
| §Grasse | 2649 | 113 | 513, 521–3, 531–3 | 0833, 1333, 1745 | |
| §Marseille | 1906 | 154 | 513, 521–3, 531–3 | 0203, 0805, 1320, 1715 | |
| Marseille | 674 | 445 | 521–2, 531–3 | 0618*, 0718, 0820, 1210†, 1830‡, 1950 | |
| France-Inter | 164 | 1829 | 513, 521–3, 531–3 | 0900, 1400, 1950 | |
| Nice | 1554 | 193 | 531–3 | 0618*, 0718. 0820. 1210†, 1830‡, 1950 | |
| Montpellier | 1403 | 214 | 521–2, 531–3 | 0618*, 0718, 0820, 1210†, 1830‡, 1950 | |
| Perpignan | 1484 | 202 | 521–3 | 0618*, 0718, 0820, 1210†, 1830‡, 1950 | |
| Monte-Carlo | 218 | 1400 | 513–33 | 0900, 2000 | Times liable to |
| Monte-Carlo | 1466 | 205 | 513–33 | 0700, 1945 | modification |
| Sud-Radio | 817 | 367 | 521–2, 531—3 | 0800, 1300, 1910 | |

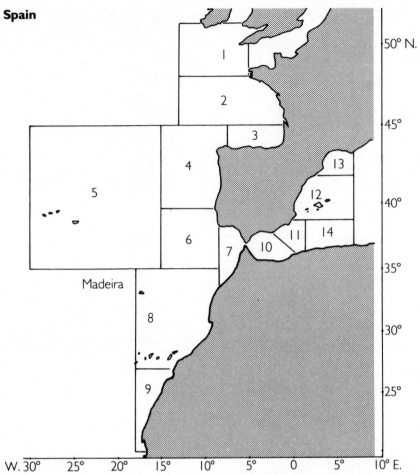

**Spain**

key
1 Gransol
2 Vizcaya
3 Cantabrico
4 Finisterre
5 Azores
6 S. Vincent
7 Cadiz
8 Canaries
9 Sahara
10 Alboran
11 Palos
12 Balearics
13 Leon
14 Argelia

| Civil Time | Stations | Frequencies | | Zones | Observations |
| | | kHz | metres | | |
|---|---|---|---|---|---|
| 1000 | Santander | 1740 | 172.4 | 1–14 | |
| 1133 | Valencia | 1680 | 178.5 | 10–12 | |
| 1303 | Santander | 1740 | 172.4 | 3 | |
| 1303 | Corunna | 1748 | 171.6 | 4 | |
| 1303 | Cadiz | 1678 | 178.8 | 7 | |
| 1303 | Alicante | 1690 | 177.5 | 10–12 | |
| 1330 | Gijon | 1730 | 173.4 | 3–6 | |
| 1403 | Barcelona | 1730 | 173.4 | 12–13 | |
| 1503 | Santander | 1740 | 172.4 | 3–4, 6–7, 10–12 | |
| 1845 | Santander | 1740 | 172.4 | 1–14 | |
| 1903 | San Sebastian | 1765 | 170 | 1–3 | Times liable to modification |

# ──Weather Forecasts──

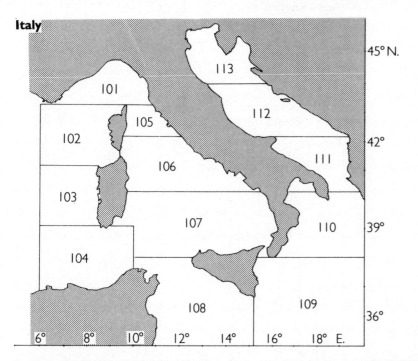

**Italy**

45° N.
42°
39°
36°

6°  8°  10°  12°  14°  16°  18°  E.

**key**
101 Ligurian Sea
102 Corsican Sea
103 Sardinian Sea
104 Sardinian Channel
105 N. Tyrrhenian
106 Central Tyrrhenian
107 S. Tyrrhenian
108 Sicilian Channel
109 S. Ionian
110 N. Ionian
111 S. Adriatic
112 Central Adriatic
113 N. Adriatic

| | Civil Time | Stations | kHz | metres | Zones | Observations |
|---|---|---|---|---|---|---|
| Times liable to modification | 0235<br>group A | Ancona Radio | 2652 | 113 | 112–113 | |
| | | Bari | 2579 | 116.3 | 110–111 | |
| | | Cagliari | 2683 | 111.8 | 103–104, 106 | |
| | | Civitavecchia | 1888 | 158.9 | 105–106 | |
| | | Genoa | 1722 | 174.2 | 101–102, 105 | |
| | | Leghorn | 2591 | 115.7 | 101, 105–106 | |
| | | Messina | 2789 | 107.5 | 107, 109–110 | |
| | | Naples | 2635 | 113.8 | 106–107 | |
| | | Palermo | 1705 | 176 | 107–108 | |
| | | Trieste | 2624 | 114.3 | 112–113 | |
| | 0250<br>group B | Crotona Radio | 2663 | 112.6 | 109–110 | |
| | | Mazara del Valle Radio | 2211 | 135.6 | 108 | |
| | | St-Benedetto del Tronto Radio | 1855 | 161.7 | 112 | |
| | | Venice | 1680 | 178.5 | 112–113 | |
| | | Augusta Radio | 1643 | 182.5 | 108–109 | |
| | 0625 | Radiodiffusione italiana | — | — | 101–113 | |
| | 0835 | Group A | — | — | See 0235 | |
| | — | Lampedusa Radio | 1876 | 160 | 108 | |
| | 0850<br>group C | Porto-Torres | 1806 | 166 | 102–103, 106 | |
| | | Trapani | 1848 | 162.3 | 107–108 | |
| | 0850 | Group B | — | — | See 0250 | |
| | 1435 | Group A | — | — | See 0235 | |
| | 1450 | Group B | — | — | See 0250 | |
| | 1535 | Radiodiffusione italiana | — | — | 101–113 | |
| | 1635 | Group C | — | — | See 0850 | |
| | 2035 | Group A | — | — | See 0235 | |
| | 2050 | Group B | — | — | See 0250 | |
| | 2050 | Group C | — | — | See 0850 | |
| | 2300 | Radiodiffusione italiana | — | — | 101–113 | |

# ── Meteorological Glossary ──
## French – English

| | |
|---|---|
| Accalmie | Lull |
| Aggravation | Deterioration |
| Alizés | Trade winds |
| Allant vers | Turning to |
| Allonger | Extend to |
| Amélioration | Improvement |
| Amplitude | Range |
| Arc en ciel blanc | Fog bow |
| Au large de | Off |
| Avec rafales | With gusts |
| Averse | Shower |
| Averse passagère | Passing shower |
| Avis | Warning |
| Avis de coup de vent | Gale warning |
| Avis de tempête | Storm warning |
| Bas | Low |
| Beau | Fair |
| Bordure | Edge |
| Brise | Breeze |
| Brise de mer | Sea breeze |
| Brise de terre | Land breeze |
| Brouillard | Fog |
| Brouillard épais | Dense fog |
| Brouillard tenu | Moderate fog |
| Brouillard très épais | Thick fog |
| Bruine | Drizzle |
| Brume | Mist |
| Brume sèche | Haze |
| Carte | Chart |
| Ceinture | Belt |
| Ceinture de hautes pressions | Belt of high pressure |
| Chaleur | Heat |
| Champ de pression | Pressure distribution |
| Changeant | Shifting |
| Ciel moutonné | Mackerel sky |
| Ciel nuageux | Scattered to broken cloud |
| Ciel peu nuageux | Scattered cloud |
| Ciel très nuageux | Broken cloud |
| Comblement d'une dépression | Filling up of a depression |
| Compte rendu | Report |
| Continu | Steady |
| Contre-alizé | Anti-trade |
| Couloir de basse pression | Neck |
| Coup de vent | Gale |
| Courant | Draft |
| Courant de perturbation | Series of disturbances |
| Courant perturbé | Disturbed stream |

# ——Meteorological Glossary——

| | |
|---|---|
| Couvert | Overcast |
| Couvert avec averses | Overcast with showers |
| Couvert avec brouillard | Overcast with fog |
| Couvert avec bruine | Overcast with drizzle |
| Couvert avec brume | Overcast with mist |
| Couvert avec neige | Overcast with snow |
| Couvert avec orage | Overcast with storm conditions |
| Couvert avec pluie | Overcast with rain |
| Creusement d'une dépression | Deepening of a depression |
| Creux dépressionnaire | Area of low pressure |
| Decroître | Decrease |
| De l'Est | Easterly |
| Dépression | Depression |
| Dernier | Last |
| Devenant très nuageux | Becoming overcast |
| Dominant | Prevailing |
| Dorsale | Ridge |
| Dorsale anticyclonique | Ridge of high pressure |
| Durer | To last |
| Ecoulement | Outflow |
| Eclair | Lightning |
| Eclaircie | Clearing |
| En formation | Developing |
| Entonnoir de trombe | Funnel cloud |
| Etabli | Settled |
| Etendre | Extend |
| Etendu | Widespread |
| Faiblissant | Falling (to) |
| Fort | Rough |
| Fraichissant | Freshening |
| Frais | Fresh |
| Front | Front |
| Front chaud | Warm front |
| Front froid | Cold front |
| Front polaire | Polar front |
| Gel | Frost |
| Gelée blanche | Hoar frost |
| Giboulée | April shower |
| Gradient | Lapse rate |
| Grain | Squall |
| Grain orageux | Thunder squall |
| Grêle | Hail |
| Grêlon | Hail stone |
| Grésii | Soft hail |
| Hausse | Rise |
| Haut | High |
| Heure d'été | Summer time |

# —— Meteorological Glossary ——

| | |
|---|---|
| Hivernage | Rainy season |
| Houle | Swell |
| Humide | Damp |
| Humidité | Moisture |
| Instable | Labile |
| Invasion | Outbreak |
| Léger | Light |
| Ligne de discontinuité | Shear line |
| Ligne de grains | Squall line |
| Lourd | Heavy |
| Marge | Flank |
| Mauvais temps | Foul weather |
| Médiocre | Poor |
| Menaçant | Lowering |
| Mer | Sea |
| Modification | Amendment |
| Moyen | Mean |
| Moyenne | Average |
| Nébulosité | Cloudiness |
| Noeuds | Knots |
| Nuage | Cloud |
| Nuageux | Cloudy |
| Obscur | Dusky |
| Ondée | Light shower |
| Orage | Thunder storm |
| Orageux | Stormy |
| Ouragan | Hurricane |
| Par moments | Now and then |
| Peu profond | Shallow |
| Pluie | Rain |
| Pluie torrentielle | Cloud burst |
| Pression | Pressure |
| Pression au niveau de la mer | Sea-level pressure |
| Prévision | Forecast |
| Prévision à longue échéance | Long-range forecast |
| Prévision plus lointaine | Further outlook |
| Probabilité | Inference |
| Profond | Deep |
| Rafale | Gust |
| Recul | Backing |
| Remous | Eddy |
| Retarder | Lag |
| Rivage | Shore |
| Route | Course |
| S'accentuer | Increase |
| S'affaiblir | Weaken |
| S'affaiser | To fall |

# Meteorological Glossary

| | |
|---|---|
| S'améliorant | Improving |
| Sans nuage | Cloudless |
| Sautes de vent | Shifts of wind |
| Se combler | Fill up |
| Se creuser | Deepen |
| Se déplacer vers | Move towards |
| S'élever | To lift |
| S'étendre | To lie, spread |
| Situation générale | Situation overall |
| Tempête | Storm |
| Temps universel | Standard Time |
| Temps variable | Unsettled |
| Tomber | To fall |
| Tonnerre | Thunder |
| Traîne | Rear (of cloud system) |
| Trajectoire | Track |
| Trombe marine | Waterspout |
| Turbulence | Gustiness |
| Vers l'Est | Eastward |
| Vers l'avant | Forward |
| Virer | Veer |
| Vraisemblable | Likely |
| Zone des calmes tropicaux | Horse latitudes |
| Zone de basses/ hautes pressions | Area of low/ high pressure |
| Zone dépressionnaire s'étendant de . . . à . . . | Area of low pressure from . . . to . . . |
| Zone sans gradient | Area of no change |

# —— Wind and Sea State ——

**Beaufort scale**

| Number | Description | | Wind speed (Knots) |
|---|---|---|---|
| | English | French | |
| 0 | Calm | Calme | < 1 |
| 1 | Light airs | Très légère brise | 1–3 |
| 2 | Slight breeze | Légère brise | 4–6 |
| 3 | Gentle breeze | Petite brise | 7–10 |
| 4 | Moderate breeze | Jolie brise | 11–16 |
| 5 | Fresh breeze | Bonne brise | 17–21 |
| 6 | Strong breeze | Vent frais | 22–27 |
| 7 | Moderate gale Near gale | Grand frais | 28–33 |
| 8 | Gale | Coup de vent | 34–40 |
| 9 | Strong gale | Fort coup de vent | 41–47 |
| 10 | Storm | Tempête | 48–55 |
| 11 | Violent storm | Violente tempête | 56–63 |
| 12 | Hurricane | Ouragan | > 64 |

**Sea state**

**Swell**

*Length:*
Short < 100 m
Medium 100–200
Long > 200

*Height:*
Slight < 2 m
Moderate 2–4
Heavy > 4

*Curvature:*
Height
─────
Length

| Code number | Description | | Height in metres |
|---|---|---|---|
| | English | French | |
| 0 | Glassy | Calme sans rides | 0 |
| 1 | Rippled | Calme ridée | 0–0.1 |
| 2 | Smooth | Belle (vaguelettes) | 0.1–0.5 |
| 3 | Slight | Peu agitée | 0.5–1.25 |
| 4 | Moderate | Agitée | 1.25–2.5 |
| 5 | Rough | Forte | 2.5–4 |
| 6 | Very rough | Très forte | 4–6 |
| 7 | High | Grosse | 6–9 |
| 8 | Very high | Très grosse | 9–14 |
| 9 | Phenomenal | Enorme | > 14 |

# ——Units of Measurement——

## Temperature

| degrees Fahrenheit | degrees Celsius |
|---|---|
| 212 | 100 |
| 194 | 90 |
| 176 | 80 |
| 158 | 70 |
| 140 | 60 |
| 122 | 50 |
| 104 | 40 |
| 86 | 30 |
| 68 | 20 |
| 50 | 10 |
| 32° F | 0° C |
| 14 | −10 |
| −4 | −20 |
| −22 | −30 |

## Pressure

| mb. | mm. |
|---|---|
| 980 | 735 |
| 985 | 738.5 |
| 990 | 742.5 |
| 995 | 746.5 |
| 1000 | 750 |
| 1005 | 754 |
| 1010 | 757.5 |
| 1013.26 | 760 |
| 1015 | 761.5 |
| 1020 | 765 |
| 1025 | 768.5 |
| 1030 | 772.5 |
| 1035 | 776.5 |
| 1040 | 780 |

1 millibar = ¾ mm mercury

$$°C = \frac{5\,(°F - 32)}{9}$$

$$°F = \frac{9 \times °C}{5} + 32$$

## Speed

| | |
|---|---|
| 1 knot | = one nautical mile per hour |
| 1 statute mile per hour | = 1609 metres per hour |

Critical speed in knots = $2.4 \sqrt{L}$ where $L$ is length on waterline in metres

## Radio

$$L \text{ (wavelength in metres)} = \frac{300{,}000}{F}, \text{ or } F = \frac{300{,}000}{L}$$

F = frequency in kilocycles or kHz

## Angles

| | | |
|---|---|---|
| 360 degrees | = | 400 grades |
| 90° | = | 8 points |
| 45° | = | 4 points |
| 11° 15′ | = | one point (approximately width of fist at arm's length) |

## Length

| | |
|---|---|
| 1 inch | = 0.0254 metres |
| 1 foot | = 0.3048 metres |
| 1 yard | = 0.9143 metres |
| 1 fathom | = 1.829 metres |
| 1 statute mile | = 1609 metres |
| 1 nautical mile (n.m.) | = 1852 metres (= 2025 yards) |
| 1 metre | = 3.28 feet |
| 1 degree | = 60 minutes |
| 1 minute | = one nautical mile |

## Volume and weight

| | |
|---|---|
| 1 gallon (English) | = 4.546 litres |
| 1 gallon (American) | = 3.785 litres |
| 1 ton (registered tonnage) | = 100 cubic feet |
| | = 2.83 cubic metres. |

Gross tonnage: volume of hull and upper works expressed in tons.

Displacement: weight of volume of water displaced (D); varies with loading. In Europe it is expressed in tons or metric tons (1000 kg).

D = volume in cubic metres × density of water.

**Geographical Coordinates**
(of a Low or High)

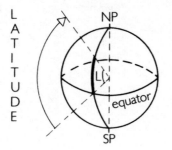

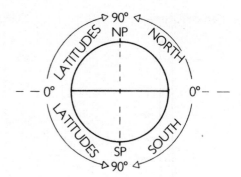

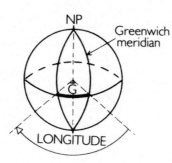

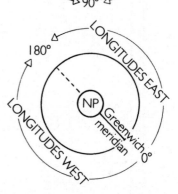

**Example**
P = 48° 51′ N. 02° 22′ E.
i.e. 48° 51′ North Latitude (measured along a meridian)
and 02° 22′ East Longitude (measured along a parallel)

*Note*
Latitude is measured from 0° to 90° and
longitude from 0° to 180°.

**Winds**

Met. forecasts always state the direction **from** which the
wind blows. (Unlike a tidal stream or current:
'southwesterly' for example, means the direction **towards**
which the current flows).

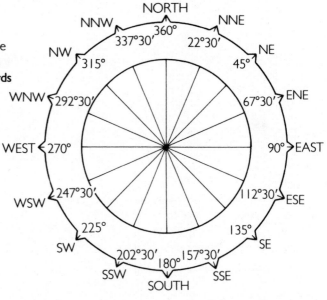

# Elementary Meteorology

**Air Masses – Winds**

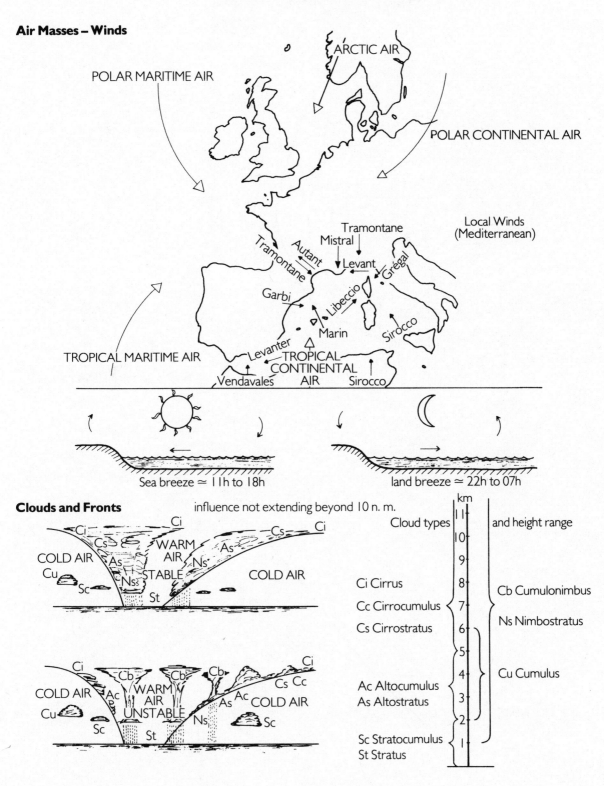

ARCTIC AIR

POLAR MARITIME AIR

POLAR CONTINENTAL AIR

Local Winds
(Mediterranean)

Tramontane
Mistral
Tramontane
Autant
Levant
Grégal
Garbi
Libeccio
Sirocco
Marin

TROPICAL MARITIME AIR

Levanter
Vendavales
TROPICAL
CONTINENTAL
AIR
Sirocco

Sea breeze ≃ 11h to 18h

land breeze ≃ 22h to 07h

**Clouds and Fronts**

influence not extending beyond 10 n. m.

Ci
Ci
Cs
Ci
COLD AIR
Cs
WARM
AIR
As
Ns
As
Ns
STABLE
COLD AIR
Cu
Sc
St

Ci
Cb
Cb
Cb
Ci
COLD AIR
Ac
WARM
AIR
UNSTABLE
As
Ac
Cs Cc
COLD AIR
Cu
Sc
Ns
St
Sc

km

Cloud types     and height range

Ci Cirrus
Cc Cirrocumulus
Cs Cirrostratus

Cb Cumulonimbus
Ns Nimbostratus

Ac Altocumulus
As Altostratus

Cu Cumulus

Sc Stratocumulus
St Stratus

# Isobars

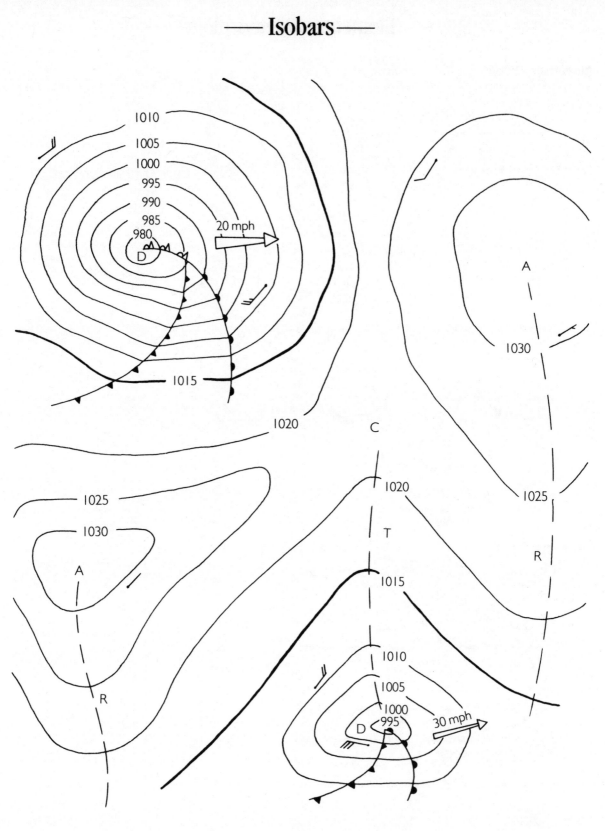

# —— Isobars ——

| | |
|---|---|
| Isobar | Line of equal barometric pressure. |
| | The standard pressure (1015 mb.) is often shown by a heavier line. |
| Anticyclone margin | Pressure zone around 1015 mb. |
| | Changeable weather, possibly misty. |
| Pressure gradient | Shown by distance between isobars. |
| | Widely separated (weak gradient) = light winds. |
| | Closely spaced (strong gradient) = strong winds. |
| Depression (D), or Low | Centre of low pressure. |
| | Generally bad weather. Wind backs (anticlockwise) |
| | in Northern Hemisphere, veers in Southern. |
| Anticyclone (A), or High | Centre of high pressure. |
| | Generally fair weather. Winds light. |
| Trough (T) | V-shaped zone of low pressure. |
| | Generally squally weather |
| Ridge (R) | U-shaped zone of high pressure. |
| | Fair weather, variable winds. |
| Col (C) | Zone with little or no pressure gradient between two highs. |
| Occlusion | Warm front lifted above the surface by advance of a cold front. |

## Symbols

| | | | | |
|---|---|---|---|---|
| 🔴🔴 | Warm front | | ◿ | Lightning |
| ▲▲ | Cold front (cold fronts faster than warm fronts). | | Ɽ | Thunderstorm |
| ⌒⌒ | Occlusion (warm front overtaken by cold front). | | , | Drizzle |
| 20 m.p.h. → | 20 mph indicating the speed and direction of movement. | | • | Rain |
| ↘ | NW. wind Force 2 (5 Knots). | | ▽ | Rain showers |
| ↗ | E. wind Force 3 (10 Knots). | | ▽ | Squall |
| ↗ | SW. wind Force 9 (45 Knots). | | ][ | Waterspout |
| ▲⟍• | W. wind Force 12 (65 Knots). | | ✳ | Snow |
| ——• | Light Westerly air (1 or 2 Knots). | | ✳▽ | Snow showers |
| = | Mist (vis. 1 mile or more) | | △▽ | Hail showers |
| ≡ | Fog (vis. less than 1 mile) | | | |

# ──Tides──

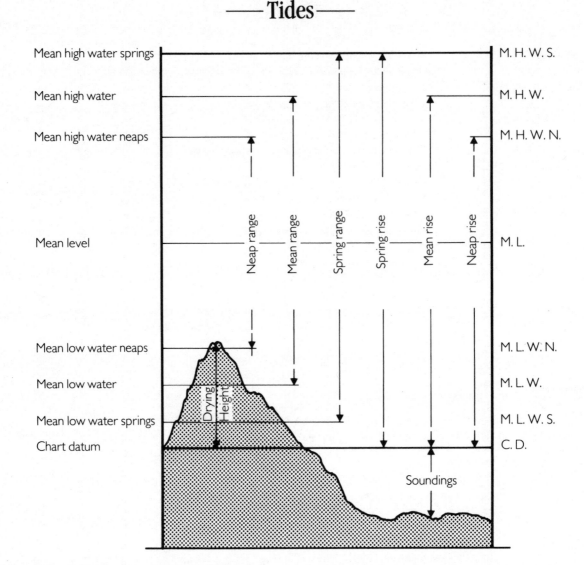

Diagram reprinted by kind permission of Reed's Nautical Almanac.

## Definitions

*Chart Datum* is approximately at the level of the lowest predictable tide (*Lowest Astronomical Tide*, LAT) although tides *may* fall below this level in some weather conditions.

*Heights and Soundings* are now shown in metres below Chart Datum, but older charts show soundings in fathoms or feet and *Drying Heights* in feet.
*Note*
The elevation of a fixed light (e. g. a Lighthouse) is the height of its focal plane above M.H.W.S., not Chart Datum.
    The elevation of a floating light (e.g. a Light vessel) is its height above sea level.

*Tidal Range* is the difference in height between H. W. and L. W. It varies from day to day and from month to month. *Spring Tides* occur a few days after the Full Moon and New Moon. *Neap Tides* are at about the Quarter Moon.

## Tide Tables

The British *Admiralty Tide Tables* show the predicted time and height of H. W. and L. W. for each day of the year for many *Standard Ports* throughout the world. Calculations for *Secondary Ports* are based on the local differences in time and height of tide in relation to a standard port.

Similar data in a more condensed form are published in *Reed's Nautical Almanac* and in local tide tables.

## Example

To find the times and heights of H.W. and L.W. at Wooton Creek with Reed's Almanac.

The *Standard Port* is Portsmouth.

| Time | | Height | |
|---|---|---|---|
| H.W. Portsmouth | 13.37 | | 4.1 m |
| Time difference | − 00.05 | Height difference | − 0.2 |
| H.W. Wooton Creek | 13.32 | | 3.9 |
| | | | |
| L.W. Portsmouth | 19.05 | | 1.4 m |
| Time difference | − 00.10 | Height difference | 0.0 |
| L.W. Wooton Creek | 18.55 | | 1.4 |

*Note*

These local time and height differences are for M. H. W. and M. L. W. and, because the difference varies during the month, the results are only approximately correct.

## Depth of Water

The soundings on a chart show depth of water above
*Chart Datum.*

    A sounding taken on board (by lead or echo sounder)
= Height of Tide + Charted Depth.
Depth of water over a Drying Shoal
= Height of Tide − Drying Height.

### Example I
Our draught is 1.2 m. and we want an under-keel
clearance of 0.5 m. when crossing the harbour bar:
What is the required *Height of Tide?*

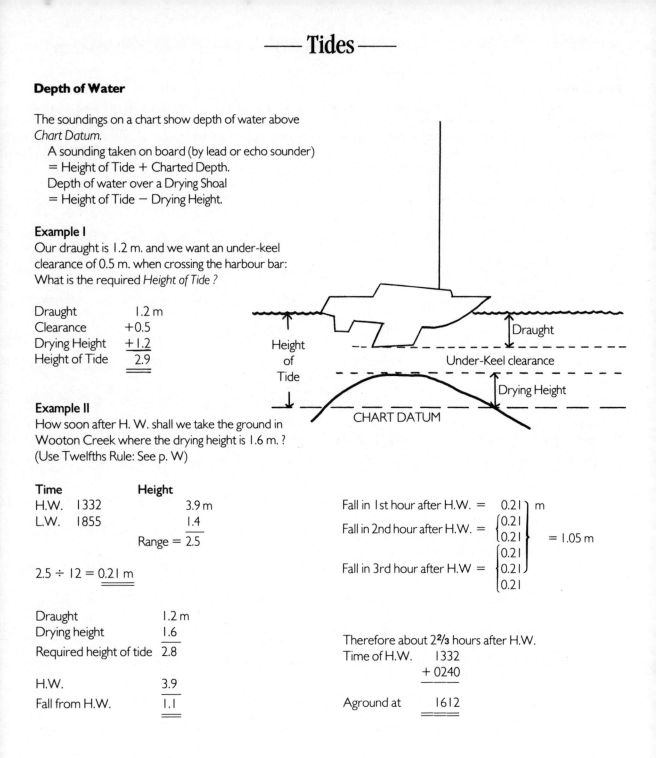

| | |
|---|---|
| Draught | 1.2 m |
| Clearance | +0.5 |
| Drying Height | +1.2 |
| Height of Tide | 2.9 |

### Example II
How soon after H. W. shall we take the ground in
Wooton Creek where the drying height is 1.6 m.?
(Use Twelfths Rule: See p. W)

| Time | | Height |
|---|---|---|
| H.W. | 1332 | 3.9 m |
| L.W. | 1855 | 1.4 |
| | | Range = 2.5 |

2.5 ÷ 12 = 0.21 m

| | |
|---|---|
| Draught | 1.2 m |
| Drying height | 1.6 |
| Required height of tide | 2.8 |

| | |
|---|---|
| H.W. | 3.9 |
| Fall from H.W. | 1.1 |

Fall in 1st hour after H.W. = 0.21 m

Fall in 2nd hour after H.W. = $\begin{cases} 0.21 \\ 0.21 \end{cases}$ = 1.05 m

Fall in 3rd hour after H.W = $\begin{cases} 0.21 \\ 0.21 \\ 0.21 \end{cases}$

Therefore about 2²/₃ hours after H.W.

| Time of H.W. | 1332 |
|---|---|
| | + 0240 |
| Aground at | 1612 |

# Tide Signals
## French ports

**I. Height of Tide** (above Chart Datum)

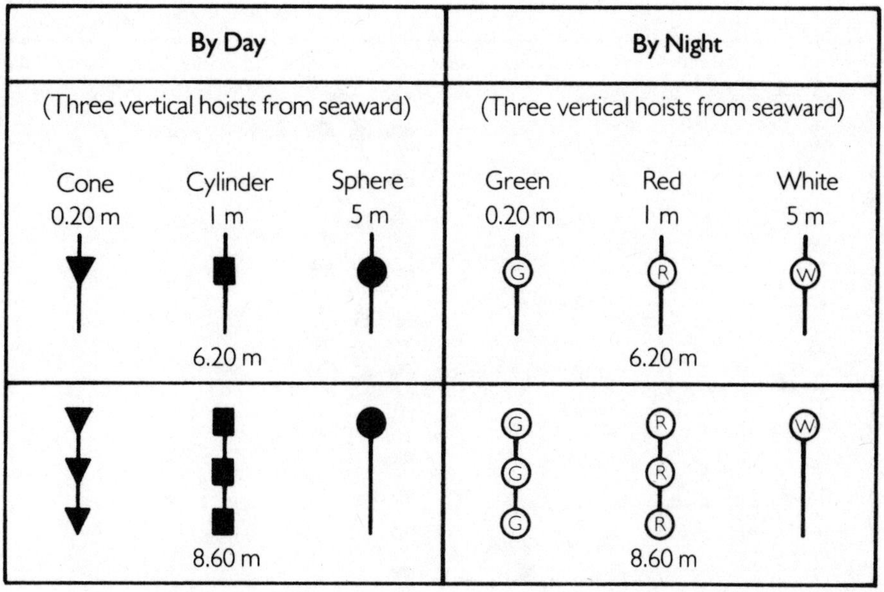

| By Day | | | By Night | | |
|---|---|---|---|---|---|
| (Three vertical hoists from seaward) | | | (Three vertical hoists from seaward) | | |
| Cone 0.20 m | Cylinder 1 m | Sphere 5 m | Green 0.20 m | Red 1 m | White 5 m |
| | 6.20 m | | | 6.20 m | |
| | 8.60 m | | | 8.60 m | |

*Note*

The shapes or lights are totalled to give the height of tide.
To indicate 0.10 m., a cylinder or red light is displayed at
the foot of, or to the left of, the left-hand mast.

**II. State of Tide**

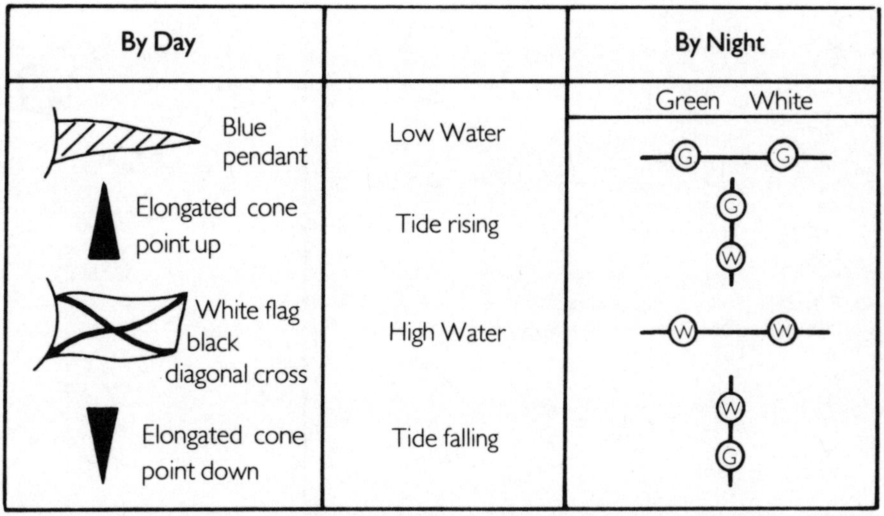

| By Day | | | By Night |
|---|---|---|---|
| | | | Green    White |
| Blue pendant | | Low Water | |
| Elongated cone point up | | Tide rising | |
| White flag black diagonal cross | | High Water | |
| Elongated cone point down | | Tide falling | |

— 25 —

# ——Chart Symbols——

## Buoys and Beacons

The complete list of symbols used on British charts is given in Admiralty Chart 5011. American chart symbols are in National Ocean Survey Chart No. 1.

|  |  | |  |  |
|---|---|---|---|---|
| | Light buoy | | | Light float |
| Bell | Bell buoy | | R B | Wreck buoy |
| Gong | Gong buoy | | | Mooring buoy |
| Whis | Whistle buoy | | RY | Practice area buoy |
| | Can buoy, Cylindrical buoy | | RY | Horizontal stripes or bands |
| | Conical buoy, Nun buoy | | BW RW BR | Vertical stripes |
| | Spherical buoy | | RW BR BW | Chequered |
| etc. | Spar buoy, floating beacon | | BR BW RW | White |
| | Pillar buoy | | W | Black |
| | Lighthouse buoy | | B | Red |
| | Spindle buoy | | R | Yellow |
| etc. | Buoy with topmark | | Y | Green |
| | Light buoy with topmark | | G | |
| | Barrel buoy, Ton buoy | | | |

Grey — Gy
Blue — Bl
Amber — Y
Orange — Or
Beacons — etc.
Beacon tower — Bn Tower, Bn Tower
Topmarks
Stake; Perch
Radar reflector
Target — Range targets, markers

## Lights

| | |
|---|---|
| ☆ | Position of important light |
| * | Position of minor light |
| Lt | Light |
| Lt Ho | Lighthouse |
| ☆ Aero | Aero light |
| ☆ | Aeromarine light |
| ☆ | Lighted beacon |
| Lt V | Light-vessel |
| F | Fixed |
| Occ | Occulting |
| Fl | Flashing |
| Iso | Isophase |
| Qk Fl | Quick flashing |
| Int Qk Fl | Interrupted quick flashing |
| Alt | Alternating |
| GpOcc | Group occulting |
| GpFl | Group flashing |
| F Fl | Fixed and flashing |
| F Gp Fl | Fixed and group flashing |
| Mo(A) | Morse code light (with flashes grouped as in letter A) |
| Vl | Violet |
| Bl | Blue |
| G | Green |
| Or | Orange |
| R | Red |
| W | White |

Red
W
Sector light
Fl.WR

Obscured
Obscured sector

# — Chart Symbols —

## Dangers

| | | | |
|---|---|---|---|
| | Rock which does not cover (with elevation above MHWS) | | Eddies |
| Dries 1.2m   *(12) | Rock which covers and uncovers (with elevation above chart datum) | | Overfalls and tide-rips |
| | Rock awash at the level of chart datum | | Breakers |
| R | Sunken rock with 2 metres or less water over it at chart datum, or | **Based on Admiralty Chart 5011** | |
| Wk | Wreck showing any portion of hull or super-structure at the level of chart datum | **Abbreviations** | |
| (Masts) (mast 3m) (Funnel) (Mast dries 2.1m) | Wreck of which the masts only are visible | Bk | Bank |
| | | Sh | Shoal |
| | Wreck over which the exact depth of water is unknown but is thought to be 28 metres or less, and which is considered dangerous to surface navigation | Rf | Reef |
| | | Le | Ledge |
| Wk | Wreck over which the depth has been obtained by sounding, but not by wire sweep | Obstn | Obstruction |
| | | Wk | Wreck |
| | Wreck over which the exact depth is unknown but thought to be more than 28 metres | dr | Dries |
| | | cov | Covers |
| | | uncov | Uncovers |
| Foul | The remains of a wreck, or other foul area, no longer dangerous to surface navigation but to be avoided by vessels anchoring, trawling etc. | (repd) | Reported |
| | | discolrd | Discoloured |
| | | (PA) | Position approximate |
| | | (PD) | Position doubtful |
| | Limiting danger line | (ED) | Existance doubtful |
| | | posn | Position |
| | | Unexamd | Unexamined |

Produced from portions of BA Chart No. 5011 with the sanction
of the Controller, H.M. Stationery Office and of the Hydrographer of
the Navy.

**Caution:** A chart which has not been brought up to date may prove of doubtful value for navigation. The Hydrographer of the Navy publishes **Notices to Mariners** weekly, listing corrections to Admiralty charts; these are obtainable from chart agents, and, in Britain, from Customs houses.

Each Notice is indexed to show at a glance which charts it affects.

# Navigation Buoys

There are five types of mark in the new IALA system:

1. *Cardinal Marks:* the deeper water is to the N. S. E. or W. of the mark (i. e. north of a North mark, etc.). Note the rhythm of the lights.
   - NORTH: a continuous series of flashes
   - EAST: group of 3 flashes ( = 3 o'clock)
   - SOUTH: group of 6 flashes ( = 6 o'clock)
   - WEST: group of 9 flashes ( = 9 o'clock)
   - Black/yellow bands; black topmark.

2. *Lateral Marks:* on the port and starboard hand in the *Conventional Buoyage Direction* (as illustrated overleaf), or when approaching a harbour or river from seaward.
   Port: red; red topmark. Starboard: green; green topmark.

3. *Isolated Danger Marks:* where there is navigable water all round the danger.
   Black/red bands; black topmark.

4. *Safe Water Marks:* where there is navigable water under the buoy as well (e. g. a mid-channel mark). Red/white bands; red topmark.

5. *Special Marks:* for special features for which you must consult the chart and sailing directions (e.g. prohibited anchorages). Yellow; yellow topmark.

**Cardinal Marks**

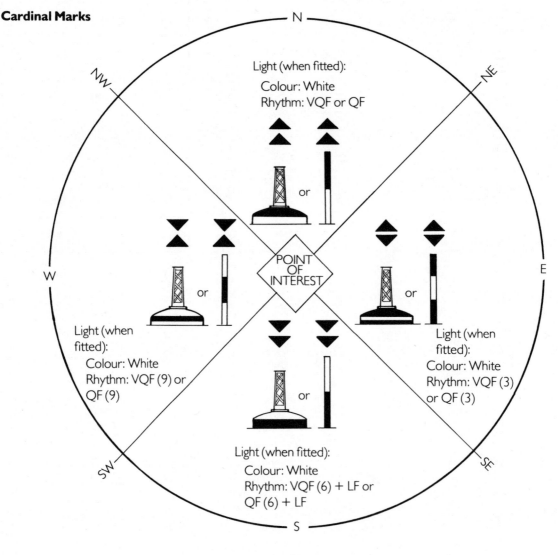

# — Navigation Buoys —

## Lateral Marks

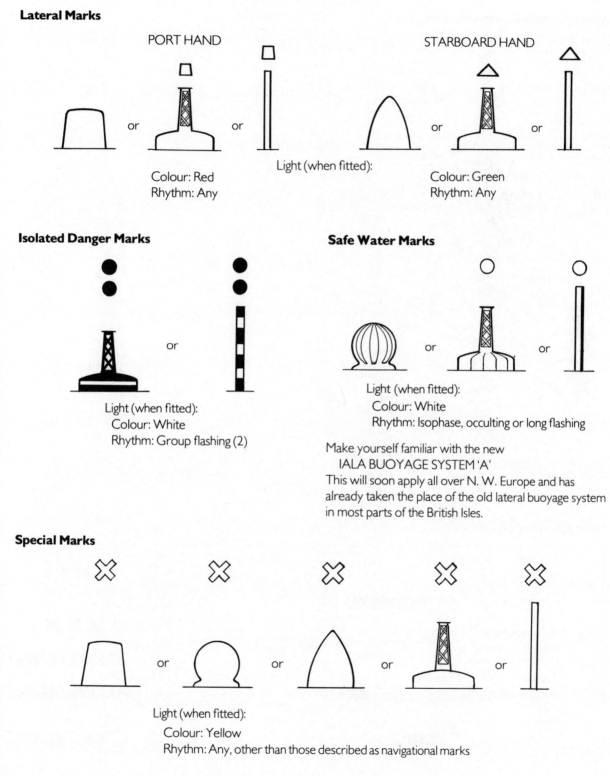

PORT HAND

or    or

Light (when fitted):

Colour: Red
Rhythm: Any

STARBOARD HAND

or    or

Colour: Green
Rhythm: Any

## Isolated Danger Marks

or

Light (when fitted):
Colour: White
Rhythm: Group flashing (2)

## Safe Water Marks

or    or

Light (when fitted):
Colour: White
Rhythm: Isophase, occulting or long flashing

Make yourself familiar with the new
IALA BUOYAGE SYSTEM 'A'
This will soon apply all over N. W. Europe and has
already taken the place of the old lateral buoyage system
in most parts of the British Isles.

## Special Marks

or    or    or    or

Light (when fitted):
Colour: Yellow
Rhythm: Any, other than those described as navigational marks

# —— Navigation Buoys ——

## Conventional buoyage direction

The direction of buoyage in rivers and estuaries is from seaward inwards.

### Flashing Codes: Buoys and Lights

| | | |
|---|---|---|
| F. | (Fixed) Continuous light. | |
| Fl. | (Flashing) Period of light less than period of dark. | |
| F.Fl. | (Fixed and Flashing) Combines both. Flash is brighter. | |
| Occ. | (Occulting) Period of dark less than period of light. | |
| Iso. | (Isophase) Period of light and dark equal. | |
| Alt. | (Alternating) Light which changes colour. | |
| Qk. Fl. | (Quick Flashing) Duration of each alternation (light + dark) is 1.0 sec. or less. | |
| Int. Qk. Fl. | (Interrupted Qk. Fl.) | |
| Gp. Int. Qk. Fl. | (Group Int. Qk. Fl.) | |
| Mo. | (Morse Code Lt) Appropriate letter/figure shown in brackets e.g. 'Mo. (B)' | |

# ——Important Checks on Gear——

(every time you go out)

## Hull

Outside:   Stanchions, life-lines and rails
              All fixed shackles secure
              Rudder, pintles and gudgeons
Below:      Calor gas
              Petrol
              Cocks (sink, W. C. etc)
              Everything properly stowed (bottles, cans etc.)

## Rigging

All halyards in good condition (in particular you don't want the mainsail to come down inadvertently!) Cross-trees properly aligned (in the two figures the stresses are equivalent)

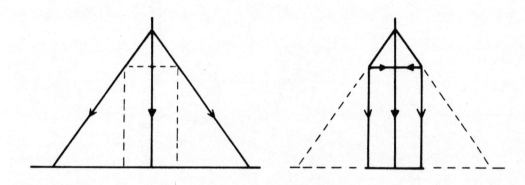

Remember the staying of the mast:
a)   Check the stepping of the mast before you leave your mooring. Shrouds and stays should be tight.
b)   At sea in a Force 3 to 4 wind check the lower shrouds and stays again. On either tack the leeward rigging should be **slack.**

*Note*
In a vessel with adjustable back-stay it should be:
   slacked off for a following wind
   tightened progressively on going more into the wind
   left slack when in port.

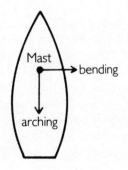

# Boat Nomenclature

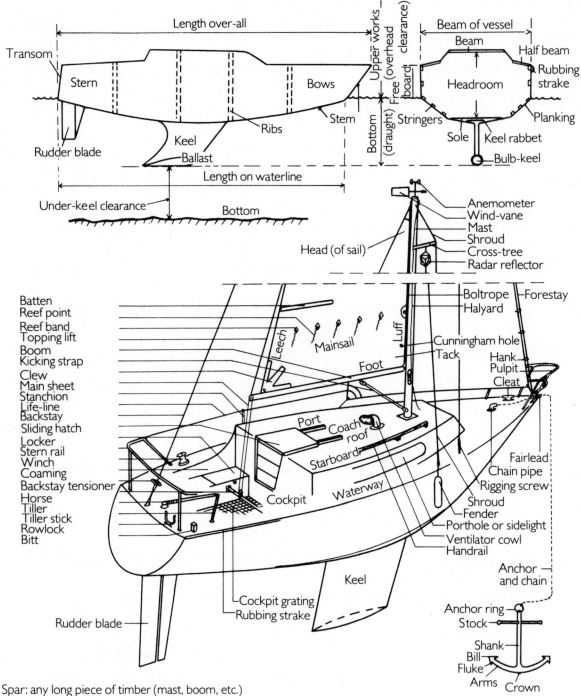

Length over-all

Transom

Stern

Bows

Stem

Ribs

Rudder blade

Keel

Ballast

Upper works

Free (overhead) clearance

board

Bottom (draught)

Under-keel clearance

Length on waterline

Bottom

Beam of vessel

Beam

Half beam

Headroom

Rubbing strake

Stringers

Sole

Keel rabbet

Planking

Bulb-keel

Anemometer
Wind-vane
Mast
Shroud
Cross-tree
Radar reflector

Head (of sail)

Boltrope — Forestay
Halyard

Batten
Reef point
Reef band
Topping lift
Boom
Kicking strap
Clew
Main sheet
Stanchion
Life-line
Backstay
Sliding hatch
Locker
Stern rail
Winch
Coaming
Backstay tensioner
Horse
Tiller
Tiller stick
Rowlock
Bitt

Leech

Mainsail

Luff

Foot

Cunningham hole
Tack

Hank
Pulpit
Cleat

Port

Coach roof

Starboard

Waterway

Cockpit

Fairlead
Chain pipe
Rigging screw

Shroud
Fender
Porthole or sidelight
Ventilator cowl
Handrail

Keel

Anchor and chain

Rudder blade

Cockpit grating
Rubbing strake

Anchor ring
Stock

Shank
Bill
Fluke
Arms    Crown

Spar: any long piece of timber (mast, boom, etc.)
Standing rigging: shrouds and stays.
Running rigging: halyards and sheets. Foresail halyards
   belayed to port, mainsail halyard to starboard.

Windlass: for weighing anchor.
Scuppers: gaps in the bulwarks to allow water to run
   off deck.

# Hull and Rig

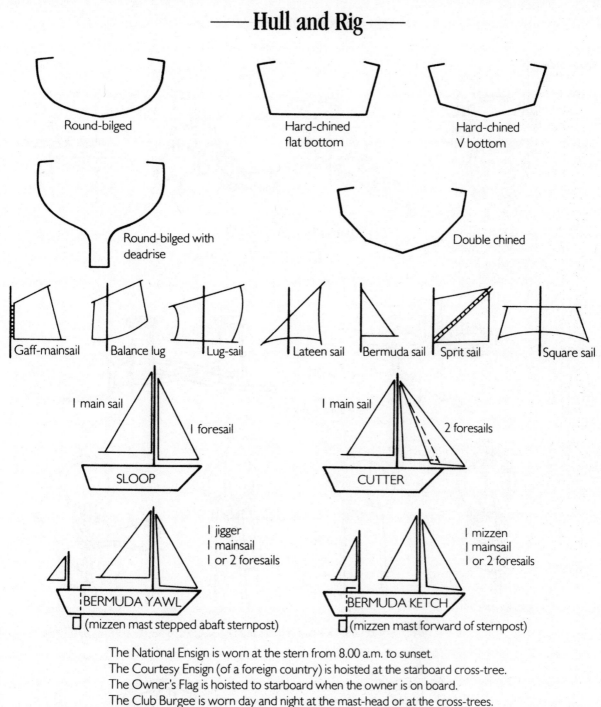

Round-bilged

Hard-chined flat bottom

Hard-chined V bottom

Round-bilged with deadrise

Double chined

Gaff-mainsail  Balance lug  Lug-sail  Lateen sail  Bermuda sail  Sprit sail  Square sail

I main sail
I foresail
SLOOP

I main sail
2 foresails
CUTTER

I jigger
I mainsail
I or 2 foresails
BERMUDA YAWL
(mizzen mast stepped abaft sternpost)

I mizzen
I mainsail
I or 2 foresails
BERMUDA KETCH
(mizzen mast forward of sternpost)

The National Ensign is worn at the stern from 8.00 a.m. to sunset.
The Courtesy Ensign (of a foreign country) is hoisted at the starboard cross-tree.
The Owner's Flag is hoisted to starboard when the owner is on board.
The Club Burgee is worn day and night at the mast-head or at the cross-trees.
Customs Clearance: By day, hoist the Code Flags D. I. F. or Q.
                By night, shine a light on the flag or
                show one red light over one white light.
The appropiate signal is to be shown continuously until the
Customs come on board and the crew can go ashore, provided that
they do not disembark any dutiable goods.

**Quayside**

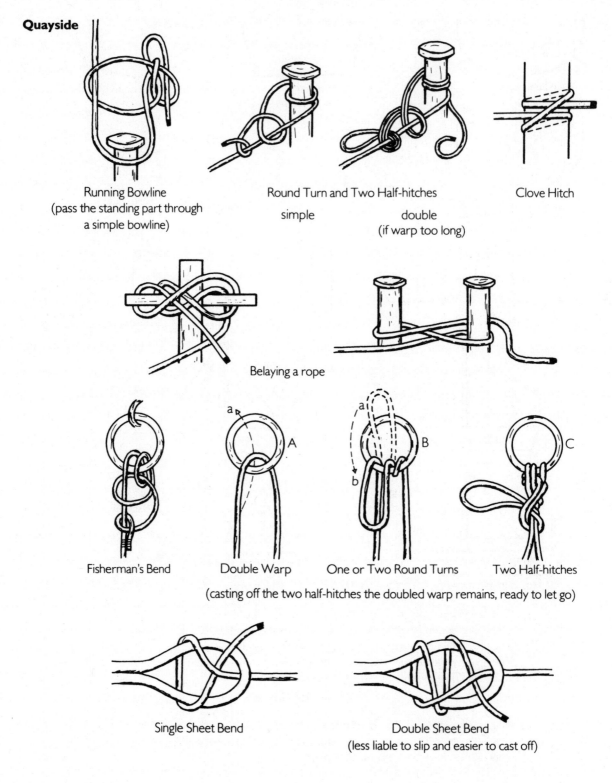

Running Bowline
(pass the standing part through
a simple bowline)

Round Turn and Two Half-hitches

simple

double
(if warp too long)

Clove Hitch

Belaying a rope

Fisherman's Bend

Double Warp

One or Two Round Turns

Two Half-hitches

(casting off the two half-hitches the doubled warp remains, ready to let go)

Single Sheet Bend

Double Sheet Bend
(less liable to slip and easier to cast off)

# — Knots —

**Aboard**

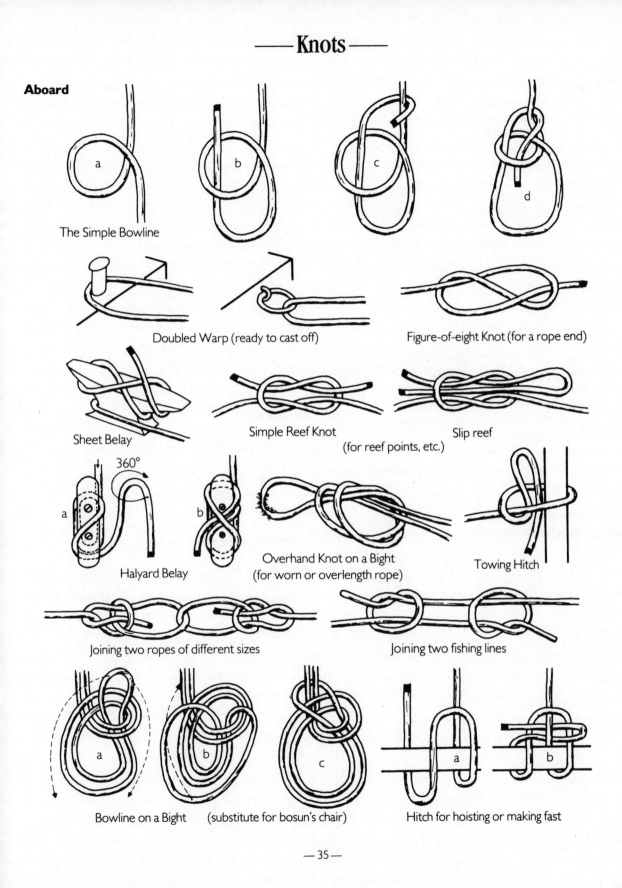

The Simple Bowline

Doubled Warp (ready to cast off)

Figure-of-eight Knot (for a rope end)

Sheet Belay

Simple Reef Knot
(for reef points, etc.)

Slip reef

360°

Halyard Belay

Overhand Knot on a Bight
(for worn or overlength rope)

Towing Hitch

Joining two ropes of different sizes

Joining two fishing lines

Bowline on a Bight     (substitute for bosun's chair)

Hitch for hoisting or making fast

## The Boat

There should always be somebody in command on board, even if the crew members are all of the same calibre.

Check the rigging and hull (look out for electrolytic corrosion). Check that the inboard end of the anchor chain is made fast, check the sea cocks, etc.

Check that all shackles are secure, check the rowlocks, the outboard motor and the free movement of the rudder.

Check the ventilation of the engine compartment (particularly with an inboard engine) before leaving your mooring.

Even a small amount of gas or petrol in the bilge will create an explosive mixture.

See that the electrical system is in good order; this may otherwise present a risk of explosion.

Fuel containers should be painted red or have a red mark. They should not be of plastic as this may induce a static charge.

No smoking when handling fuel or sails.

Outboard motors for use at sea should have a separate fuel tank, not attached to the engine.

A paraffin hurricane lamp is safe and indispensable.

Life-jackets should always be at hand and should never be used as cushions or pillows as this reduces their volume and buoyancy.

Be thoroughly familiar with the equipment for distress signals : in particular the use of a mirror for heliograph signals.

A jerrycan of water three-quarters full will float.

Before correcting your compass see that all metal objects (chains, jerrycans, tools etc.) are stowed in their usual places.

Observe this rule particularly when navigating in fog.

Keep everything ship-shape. It should be possible to find anything immediately, without delay, especially at night.

Sail ties neatly coiled ready to hand.

See that accumulators are well ventilated (as they give off hydrogen when charging) and secure them so that they are not in direct contact with the hull.

A rope ladder is not a luxury (man overboard, etc.)

Always wear shoes or sea boots.

The shrouds should never be used for getting on board, going over the side or hoisting gear.

The inboard end of the cable should be made fast with a seizing and never with a shackle.

The fixed life-lines must be secured to the pulpit and stern rail with nylon or terylene lanyards to avoid interference with the D. F. apparatus.

Make a check list of things to be seen to before departure and on return to port.

## The Dinghy

For greater stability keep the centre of gravity low: sit in the bottom of the boat.

When taking to a life-raft do not forget to take enough line with you to use for towing, for a drogue, for safety harnesses, life-lines etc.

If you are in the water put your arms through the life-lines, do not hold on with your hands.

### Distress Signals

SOS ( · · · --- · · ·) 500 kHz (600 m) by radio telegraph.

Radio silence: 15 and 45 minutes past each hour.

MAYDAY 2182 kHz (137.5 m) by radio telephone.

Radio silence: on the hour and 30 minutes past.

## The Sea

Never set sail without knowing the weather situation.

Choose a day with moderate wind for the first sail of the season.

If a passage is likely to be of any length inform one of your friends and give him the particulars of the boat (name, type and sail number).

All preparations for a serious voyage should be completed ashore.

The passage plan should allow plenty of flexibility.

In Britain contact H. M. Coastguard for passage surveillance (Form CG 66A and B).

Speeds in excess of 5 kt. are prohibited within 300 metres offshore in French waters.

If you have to cross a recognised traffic lane do so as nearly as practicable at right angles to the traffic.

Vessels with a diver down display the International Code Signal 'A' (a blue and white flag) or a red flag with a white diagonal cross. Pass at a distance of at least 50 metres and with caution.

Go to the assistance of any vessel making the 'N C' signal, the 'V' signal, red flares or a MAYDAY call.

The unjustified use of distress signals is an offence.

It is illegal to moor to navigation buoys.

No crew member should go barefoot when handling chain cables.

Dinghy helmsman should never use teeth when sheeting in.

When running, the boom must not be allowed to touch the shrouds and the main sheet should be cleated on the same side; an involuntary gybe could be fatal to masts and spars.

A rope should be belayed to a cleat; avoid a half-hitch.

A lifting rudder blade may break if used at an angle of more than 45°.

In a strong wind plastic sail battens are better.

Keep clear of shoals in a big sea.

Provide yourself with a suitable boat knife.

Do not tow a rubber dinghy on a long painter: painter may part.

Where there is only a small under-keel clearance, only skirt the shore on a rising tide.

At night wear your life-jacket, safety-harness and a water-proof torch, especially in a strong wind or with the spinnaker up.

At night do not use an electric torch near the compass; very few batteries are non-magnetic.

At night, even with navigation lights, when close hauled under jib or genoa (which may obscure the view to leeward) you may be in risk of collision with a yacht on the other tack, close hauled and sailing at the same speed. So watch out!

When moored for the night put your ladder over the side in case someone falls overboard while the crew is asleep.

In heavy weather do not use frying pans or long-handled saucepans. The cook should wear trousers over boots.

If a gas burner goes out while you are cooking allow maximum ventilation before you relight it.

Hunger, fatigue and cold are the cruising sailor's worst enemies.

Confusion and lack of discipline are the main source of dangerous situations.

It is the skipper who shoulders legal responsibilities.

# —— Port Entry and Departure Signals ——
## French Ports

| Simplified Code | By Day | | By Night |
|---|---|---|---|

**Colour Code**
B.    blue
R.    red
G.    green

Entry Prohibited
(departure permitted)

Departure Prohibited
(entry permitted)

Entry and Departure
Prohibited

## Special Supplementary Signals

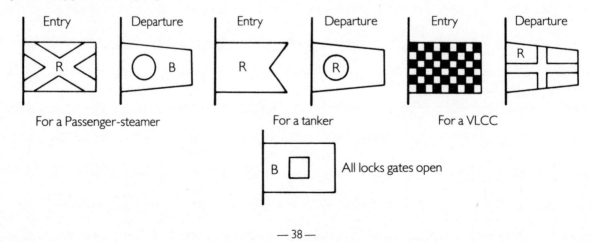

Entry    Departure      Entry    Departure      Entry    Departure

For a Passenger-steamer      For a tanker      For a VLCC

All locks gates open

# Port Entry and Departure Signals

**French Ports**

## Normal Operation

**By Day**
          **By Night**

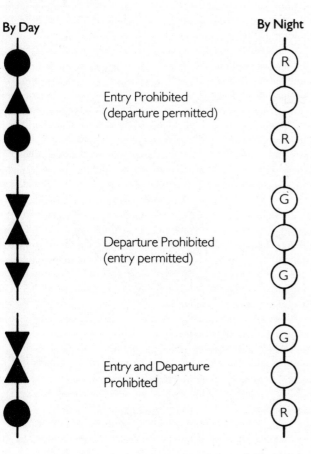

Entry Prohibited
(departure permitted)

Departure Prohibited
(entry permitted)

Entry and Departure
Prohibited

## Emergency

Port Closed
Entry absolutely prohibited

Port Open
May mean
obstructions in channels so
proceed with caution

# — Points of Sailing —

Wind direction?
Judge from burgee or wind-vane
Wind on your face: when loudest wind-sound is
equal in both ears you are facing wind.

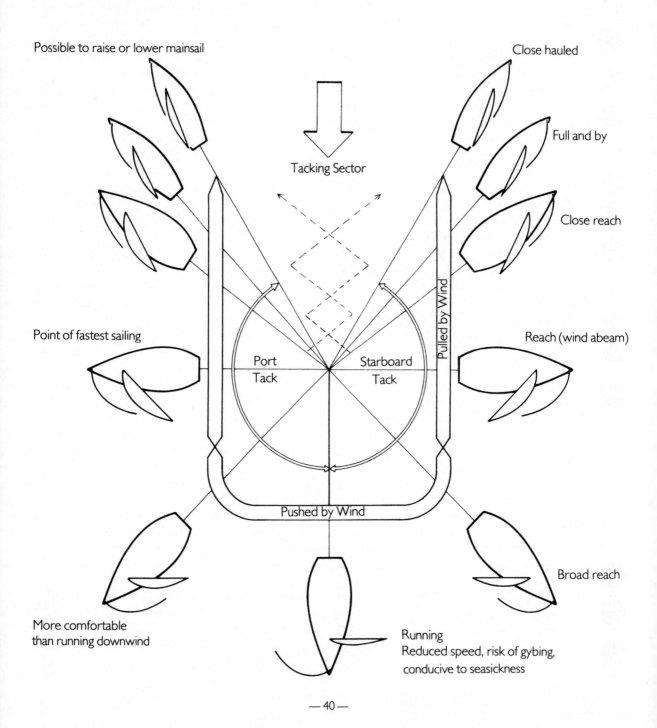

Possible to raise or lower mainsail

Close hauled

Full and by

Close reach

Tacking Sector

Point of fastest sailing

Reach (wind abeam)

Pulled by Wind

Port
Tack

Starboard
Tack

Pushed by Wind

More comfortable
than running downwind

Broad reach

Running
Reduced speed, risk of gybing,
conducive to seasickness

# Balance

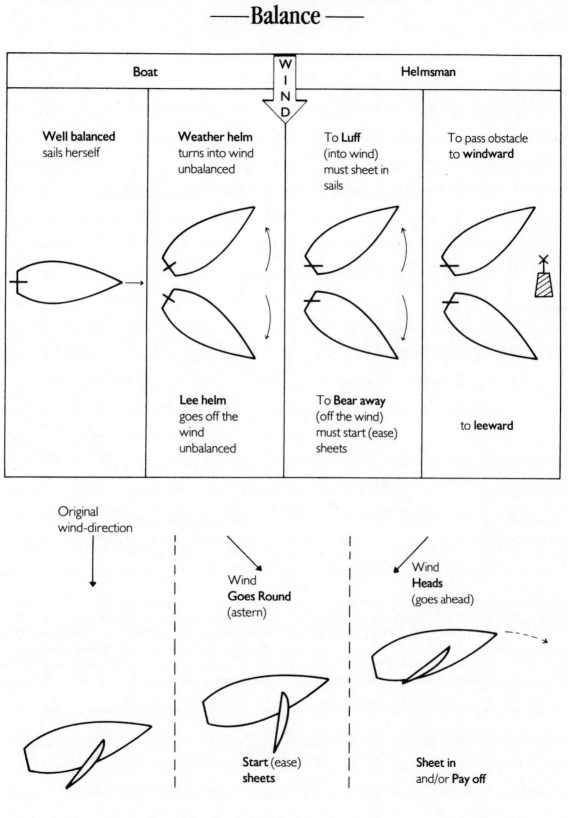

| Boat | | WIND | Helmsman | |
|---|---|---|---|---|
| **Well balanced** sails herself | **Weather helm** turns into wind unbalanced | To **Luff** (into wind) must sheet in sails | To pass obstacle to **windward** |
| | **Lee helm** goes off the wind unbalanced | To **Bear away** (off the wind) must start (ease) sheets | to **leeward** |

Original wind-direction

Wind **Goes Round** (astern)

Wind **Heads** (goes ahead)

**Start** (ease) sheets

**Sheet in** and/or **Pay off**

**Wind on the Bow**

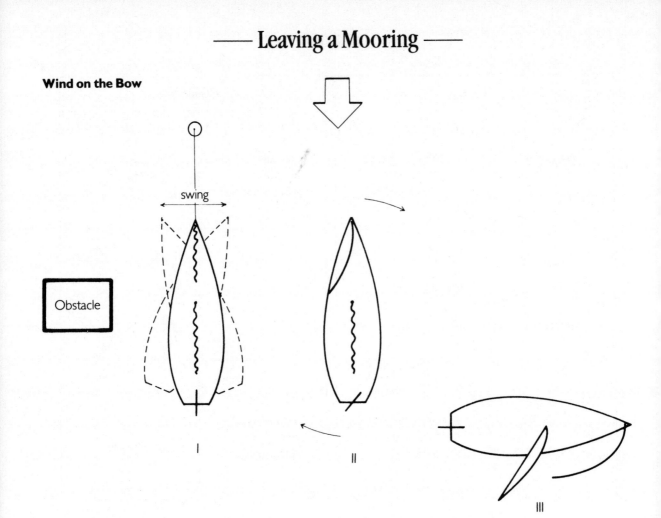

I. Hoist mainsail (sheet let out fully).
Hoist jib (sheet slack).
Note:
    The swing. (A boat at a mooring is seldom still.)
    The obstacle, whether fixed or last-minute. (As this
    obstacle is to port, you get away to starboard.)

II. The helm is put over 45° to **starboard.** (When you
cast off, the boat will go astern and the rudder has
opposite effect.)
Cast off mooring when boat swings to starboard.
Harden up port jib sheet. (In light airs bring jib over by
hand with tack over the side.)

III. Sheet in the sails as far as possible. (Too much and you
get into irons, see p. N.)
Helm amidships.

**Caution**
Leaving a mooring, when the boat has no way on, she
makes **least** leeway with the wind abeam, so keep on this
course for ten yards or so to make headway before you
luff up. Make sure therefore that you have **enough water
under your lee.**

# —— Leaving a Mooring ——

**Wind Astern**

Mooring is in strong current flowing against the wind.

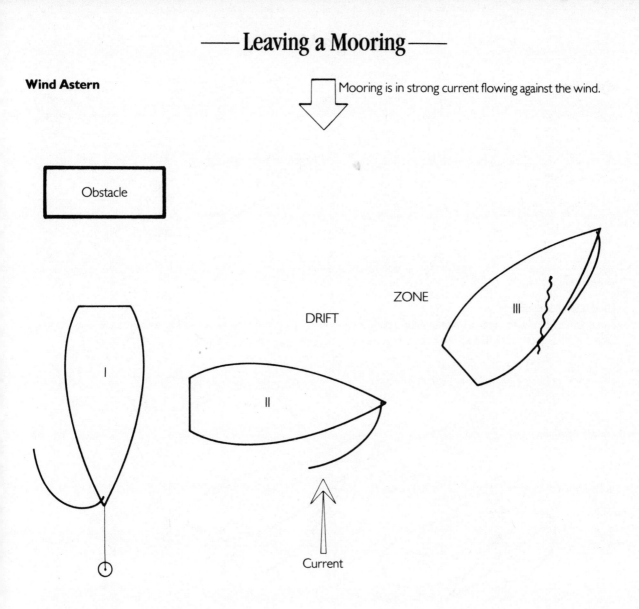

Obstacle

ZONE

DRIFT

I

II

III

Current

I. Hoist the jib.
Have mainsail ready to hoist.
With jib up, the mooring will show you whether you are stemming the current. You can later hoist the genoa instead.

II. Cast off. Make sure you have **enough water downstream.**

III. Hoist the mainsail when you are on a close reach.

## Wind Across Current

(a sample case)

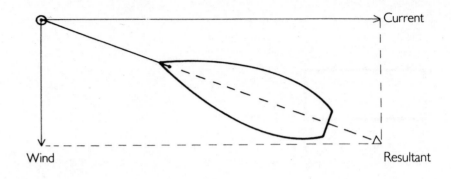

Wind                                        Resultant

**Theoretical situation:**

The effect of the water against the hull, keel and rudder differs from the effect of the wind on the top sides and rigging. The boat answers helm (due to the effect of the current on the rudder).

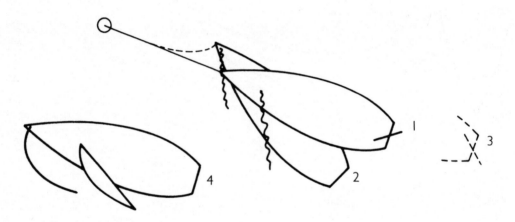

1. Helm a-lee: with the wind too much abeam it is difficult to hoist mainsail. Use rudder to bring boat to position (2).
2. Hoist mainsail and then jib.
3. Come back to position (1) by putting helm to windward. **Harden in** sheets and **cast off.**

*Note*
Do not cast off in position (2) or current may swing you round.

# —— Leaving a Mooring ——

## Weighing anchor

**Preparatory:**

1. Hoist mainsail. (Let out sheet.)
2. The jib (ready to hoist) remains lowered while anchor is being hove in, particularly if wind strong.

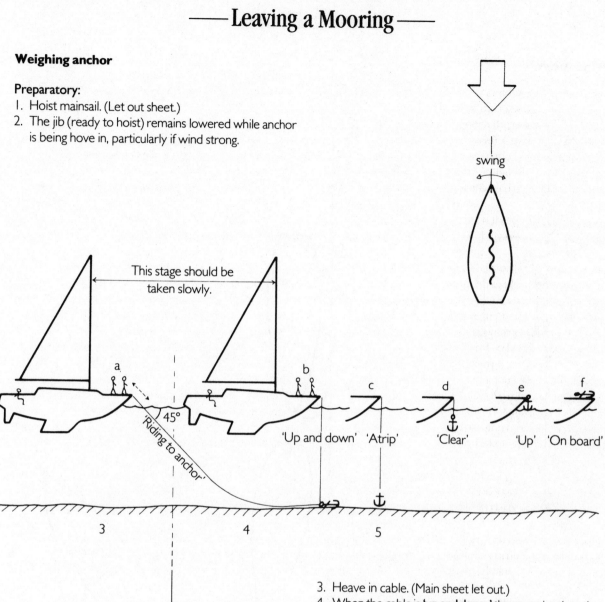

3. Heave in cable. (Main sheet let out.)
4. When the cable is **'up and down'** the crew signals to the helmsman: anchor no longer holds and vessel liable to come adrift and make sternway.
5. The crew signals **'atrip'**. The cable is then quickly hove in: vessel now gathering sternway. (Don't let the anchor scrape under the hull.)

If **obstruction** should appear to leeward, stand by, on skipper's or helmsman's order, to cast anchor again — particularly at the decisive **'up and down'** stage.

**Preliminary note:**

The sheer (to port and starboard) when cable is 'up and down' will help you decide which tack to sail on.

**In heavy weather** the bow lifts and falls with the seas. The cable is hove in as she plunges to spare the labour of two crew men, or even three on occasion.

# — Leaving a Quay —

**Wind Astern**

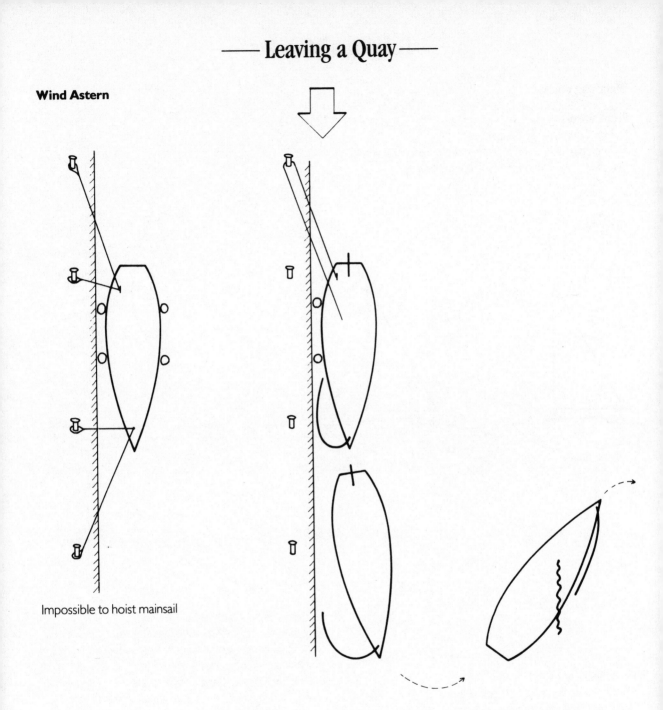

Impossible to hoist mainsail

Hold the stern rope: should be a doubled warp.
Hoist jib. Mainsail ready to hoist.
Cast off warp, let boat gather way.
Turn to windward and hoist mainsail.
Set boat on course.

# — Leaving a Quay —

**Wind Ahead**

GOING ASTERN

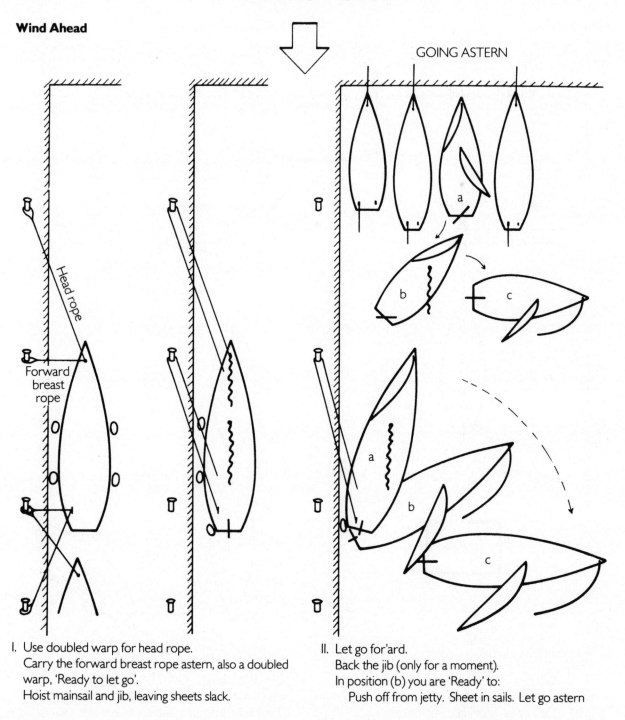

I. Use doubled warp for head rope.
   Carry the forward breast rope astern, also a doubled warp, 'Ready to let go'.
   Hoist mainsail and jib, leaving sheets slack.

**Going astern**
Put jib and mainsail aback. If departure to starboard, both mainsail and tiller should be to starboard. **Alternatively,** if

II. Let go for'ard.
   Back the jib (only for a moment).
   In position (b) you are 'Ready' to:
      Push off from jetty.  Sheet in sails.  Let go astern

there is enough room to leeward go astern 'under bare poles'; the boat will then turn down-wind. Hoist the jib, round up into wind again and hoist mainsail.

# —— Leaving a Quay ——

**Wind Abeam**

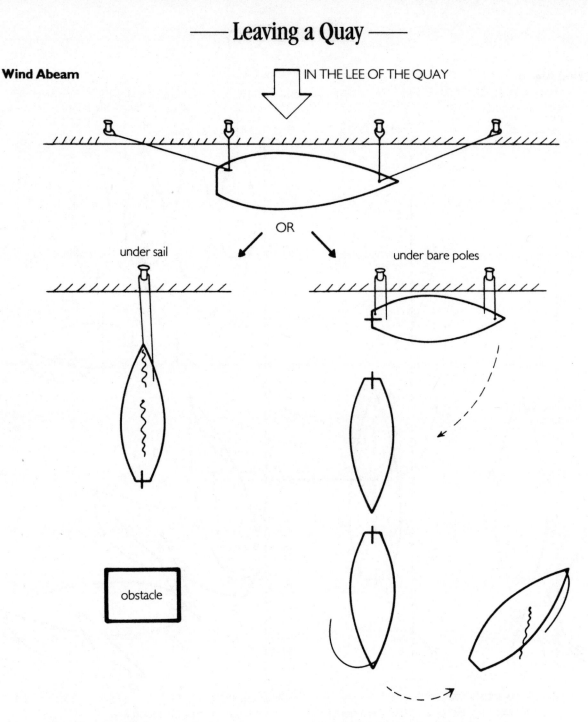

IN THE LEE OF THE QUAY

OR

under sail

under bare poles

obstacle

Stand by a doubled warp at the bow.
Hoist mainsail and jib.
Cast off (as on p. 42)

Cast off, first forward and then astern.
When wind is astern, hoist jib.
Come round into wind and hoist mainsail.

# —— Leaving a Jetty ——

**Wind Abeam**

TO WINDWARD OF JETTY

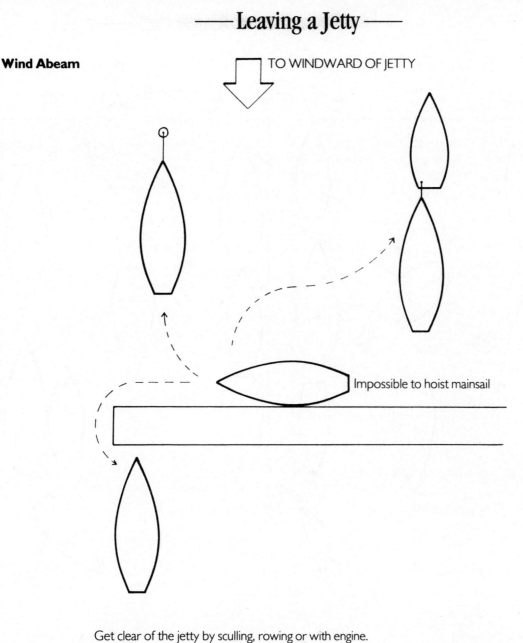

Impossible to hoist mainsail

Get clear of the jetty by sculling, rowing or with engine.
Pick up a buoy or moor to stern of another vessel.
It may be possible to get to leeward of jetty by warping boat along to the end.
Hoist mainsail and jib.

# Leaving a Pontoon

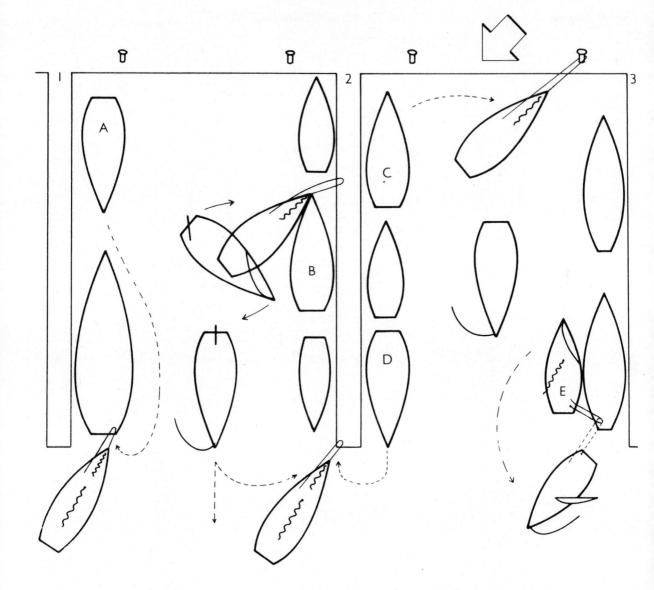

A and D On the windward side of pontoon, impossible to
hoist mainsail.
Warp along and moor to stern of last boat in the
row, or to end of pontoon.
Hoist the mainsail and jib.
B To leeward of pontoon.
If there is much wind hoist only the jib; with
mainsail up the boat would have too much
weather helm (p.T) and risk hitting No. 2
Pontoon.

Cast off, with jib aback and helm to leeward.
C Warp boat along to most windward of the
bollards.
Now proceed as under B above.
E Double-moored to leeward of pontoon and
near the end.
Hoist mainsail and jib.
Cast off forward with jib aback and let boat
swing round.
Cast off astern.

# ──Leaving a Pontoon──

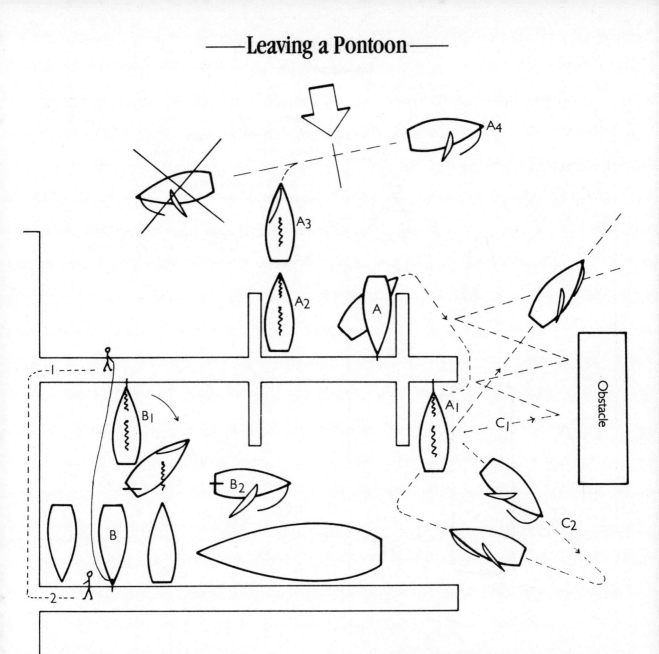

A2 (second alternative)
 With wind on port bow, A4 is the better course.
 Since berth A2 is vacant, work her over to that and
 hoist sail.
 Crew members on the pontoon push off (A3); put
 her off the wind with jib slightly aback.

A1 (first alternative)
 Turn boat end for end.
 Warp her round pontoon to position A1.
 Hoist mainsail and jib.
 Manoeuvre C1 will require several short tacks with
 little way on the boat and risk of getting into irons.
 Manoeuvre C2 will get you back to position A1
 with plenty of way on the boat.

B One of the crew takes a light warp round to No. 1
 Pontoon, makes end fast to a bollard and throws warp
 back to B. The boat is warped over to B1 where jib and
 mainsail can be hoisted since at B2 wind will be abeam.

# —Navigating a Channel—
## On a close reach

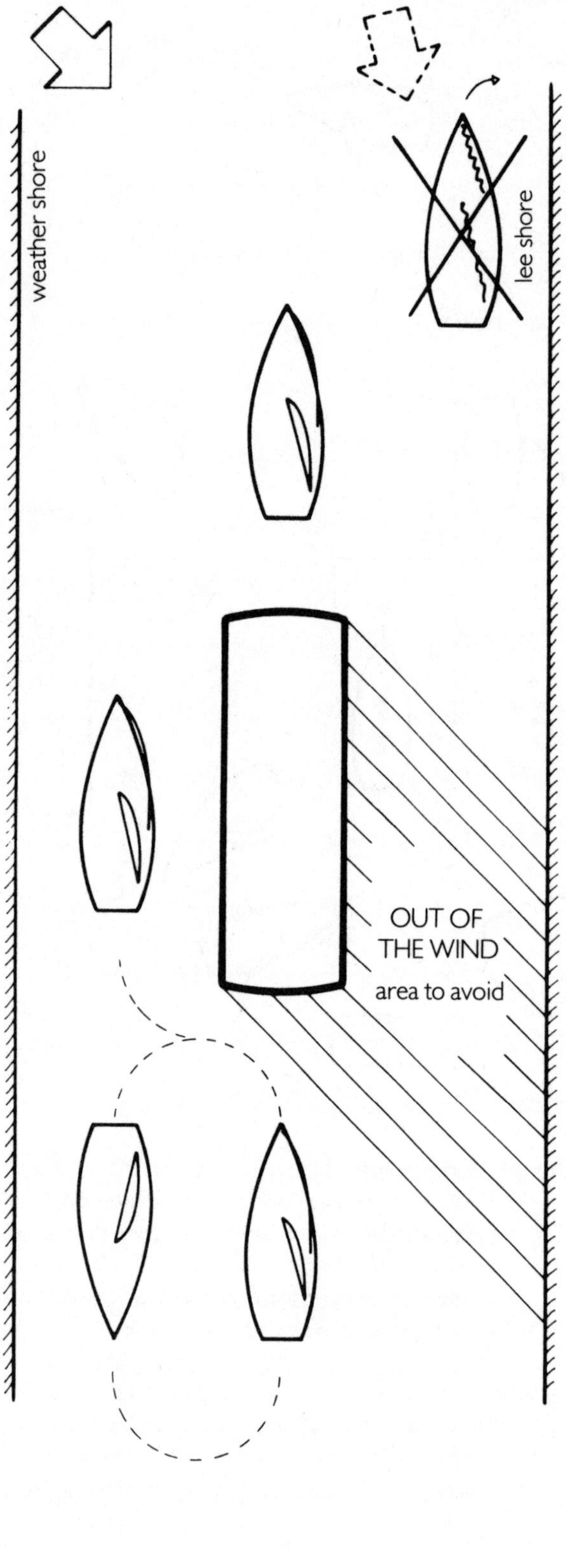

weather shore

lee shore

OUT OF
THE WIND
area to avoid

In theory keep to starboard (off the lee shore in this case).
**But if** the wind drops **and** the helmsman is inexperienced
you risk **running aground.**
**Therefore** wiser to keep to the middle.

**If a ship approaches**, ahead or astern, keep to the
**windward** of her.

If there is much traffic make a 180° turn with mainsail
sheeted in and jib lowered (**to reduce speed**).
**When the way is clear**, resume course.

# — Navigating a Channel (or River)—

### Where channel narrows

There is more wind.
The waves are shorter and steeper (particularly if wind against current).

### Keep to the middle

If you have to stop you can turn either to port or starboard.

### Under bare poles

Less wind resistance.
Have jib ready to hoist.

### Never set your mainsail

If engine stops with mainsail up, you will carry weather helm (p. T) and it will be difficult to put wind astern. Risk of grounding.

### Engine failure or cavitation

Immediately: Hoist jib.
Turn down-wind.
Then hoist mainsail if you wish, while making a 360° turn, and run before the wind.

# —— Sculling ——

To understand this section get yourself a scull or, at home,
a broomstick.

**Position**

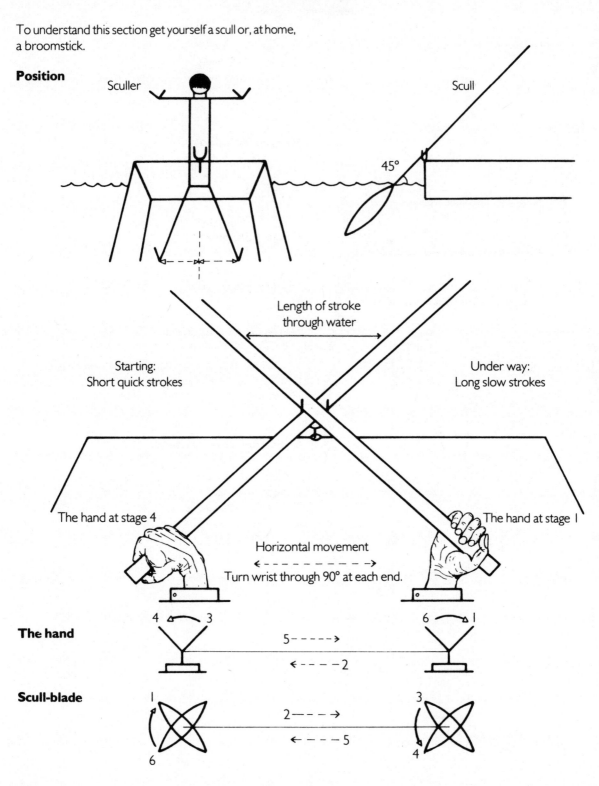

Sculler

Scull

45°

Length of stroke
through water

Starting:
Short quick strokes

Under way:
Long slow strokes

The hand at stage 4

The hand at stage 1

Horizontal movement
Turn wrist through 90° at each end.

**The hand**

4 ⌂ 3          6 ⌂ 1

5 - - - - - →

← - - - - 2

**Scull-blade**

1          3

2 - - - →

← - - - 5

6          4

# ——Inflatable Dinghies——

## Inflation

Non-automatic (with foot pump), for use as tender, for picking up mooring, etc.
Automatic, as a life-raft.

Secured to the boat by its painter, the raft is thrown overboard and inflates automatically. (Keep a steady pull on the painter to ensure that gas bottle opens.)

There should be knife in dinghy to cut the painter.
A sailor always carries a good knife, in case dinghy knife mislaid.

## Propulsion

**Rowing:**  Two oars (or paddles).
**Paddling:**  Two paddles, or more if there are more persons on board.
**Sculling:**  A scull (or paddle).

**Paddling at the bow:**  A paddle or scull at the bow allows you, when single-handed, to go upwind. (When sculling, the dinghy up-ends and is caught by the wind.)

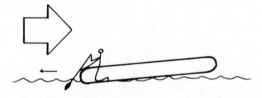

Kneeling, one arm bent, the other lightly extended.

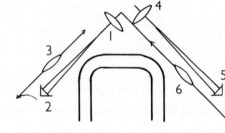

The blade strokes from side to side. Wrists turn through 90° at stages 2 and 5.

## In use

a) **To carry people:**  They should sit in the bottom to lower the centre of gravity and increase stability.

b) **To put out a cable or warp:**  All to be piled in dinghy, not on board yacht.

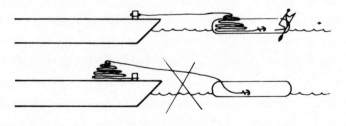

# —— Sails – Heading – Helm ——

## a) Trimming sail

The mainsheet horse:
> In light airs, traveller amidships.
> In a strong wind, traveller to leeward.
> Wind astern, traveller amidships.

The trim when close-hauled:
1. Jib well sheeted in.
2. Put her up into the wind until mainsail begins to lift along the luff; then put her a little off the wind till this stops.
3. Let out the mainsail and then sheet it in as far as possible. Sheet mainsail in lightly if air-flow off jib lifts it.

> Tightening the **foot** of the sail will reduce its curvature. Tightening the **luff** will prevent the hollow of the sail from moving aft (Cunningham hole).

## b) Keeping on course

1. Note course ordered by navigator.
2. Ease jib and then sheet in as much as possible.
3. Ease and sheet in mainsail.

## c) Steering

A good helmsman 'follows the helm'; he does not snatch at it but follows its swing, within limits.
**Visual:** When sailing on a mark allow for parallax (parallel to axis of boat from steering position).
If you are not sailing on a mark, keep the pulpit steady on horizon.

**By compass:** Note course and then steer by eye. Check compass course from time to time.

NEVER STEER WITH YOUR EYE GLUED TO THE COMPASS.

# — Sundry Observations —

**Helmsmanship in rough weather:**

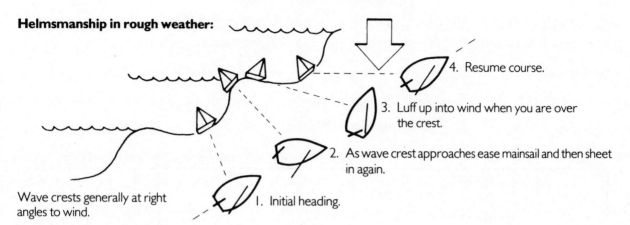

4. Resume course.

3. Luff up into wind when you are over the crest.

2. As wave crest approaches ease mainsail and then sheet in again.

1. Initial heading.

Wave crests generally at right angles to wind.

**Breaking waves:**   When going to windward take the breakers head-on if you can. The crest of a breaker is a mixture of water and air: boat loses some of her buoyancy.

**Going on the other tack:**   You may not be able to tack (if carrying too much canvas or in a heavy sea).

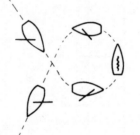

If the helmsman is afraid to gybe he can put her up into wind and tack round.

Try tacking in the trough of a wave, or wear round, stern to wind.

**A buoy** should be picked up from below,

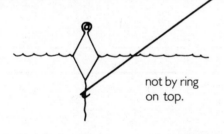

not by ring on top.

**The sea anchor:** Do not forget tripping line to capsize and retrieve anchor.

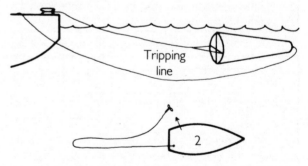

Tripping line

How to stream **log**.

**When tacking** to windward, helmsman will find it easier in most boats with tiller if he faces the stern when shifting himself across boat.

**Beating to windward:**  you cover twice the distance made good, and it takes you three times as long, as it would down wind.

**Changing jibs** should be practised with the wind astern.

**The lead-line** should be in a bucket, not coiled, and the end made fast.

# ——Watches——

Length of a watch should not exceed 4 hours.
Each watch should in general include two or three of the crew, to cover working the boat and all other duties on board (cleaning, cooking, etc.).

Some examples:

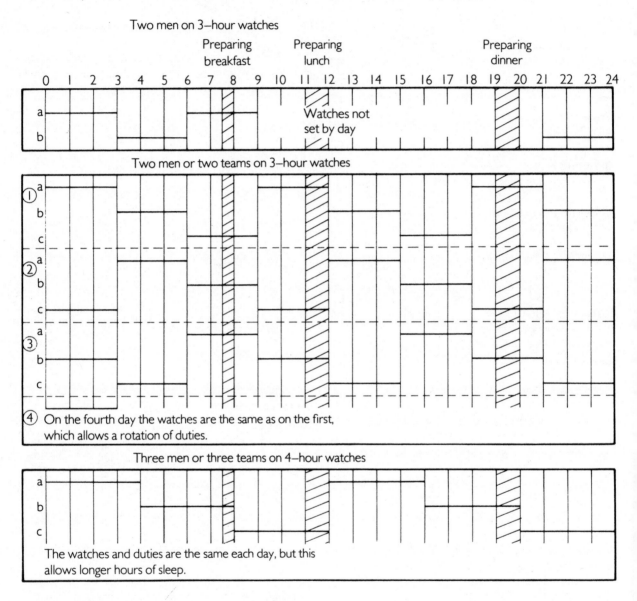

The watches and duties are the same each day, but this allows longer hours of sleep.

You can work out many other duty rosters, taking into account each man's competence in navigation, cooking, odd jobs, etc.

The skipper is always on call, but in principle he does not keep a watch.

The watch is called a quarter of an hour before taking over and is given all instructions.

At night everyone on deck is to wear a safety-harness.

# ——Tidal Streams——

Consult the **Sailing Directions**, or the insets on the chart, for:

Direction in which stream sets in relation to True North.
Rate of stream, in knots and tenths.
Time before or after H.W.

This information is given for hours before and after High Water at the Standard Port.

**Tide rose**

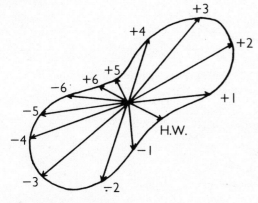

– I means one hour before High Water.
+ 3 means three hours after High Water.

When written over an arrow:

2h. of ebb, means 2 hours after ebb begins.
4h. of flood, means 4 hours after flood begins.

**Tabular presentation**

**Written out:**
a) −0330 Dover means 3 h. 30 m. before H. W. Dover.
b) A rate without indication of Springs or Neaps refers to Mean Springs.

**In Tidal Atlas:**
14.08 over arrow means 1.4 knots at Springs and 0.8 knots at Neaps; the arrow shows the direction.

Standard Port

| Reference Number | 335 | | |
|---|---|---|---|
| Geographical Position | Lat     48°42′5N. | | |
|  | Long    1°59′5W. | | |
| Time | Direction in degrees | Mean Rate | |
|  |  | Springs (Knots) | Neaps (Knots) |
| −6 . . . . . . . . . . . . . . | 241 | 0.6 | 0.3 |
| −5 . . . . . . . . . . . . . . | 119 | 0.4 | 0.2 |
| −4 . . . . . . . . . . . . . . |  |  |  |
| −3 |  |  |  |
| −2 |  |  |  |
| − I | – | – | – |
| H.W. |  |  |  |
| + I |  |  |  |
| +2 |  |  |  |
| +3 |  |  |  |
| +4 |  |  |  |
| +5 |  |  |  |
| +6 |  |  |  |

A dash means that the rate has not been determined.

# — Tidal Streams —

## Rate of stream

Greatest (usually) at half-tide.
Increases with tidal range.
Increases with wind force.
Increases in narrow channel.

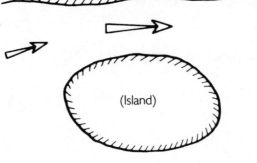

Venturi effect

(Island)

Decreases at neap tide (beginners can take advantage of this).

Decreases when wind and tide are opposed.
Decreases close inshore.

H   deep water
h   shallows (banks)

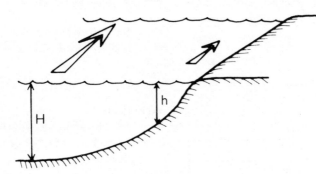

*Note*
There may be breaking waves over bank.

## Sea state

WIND

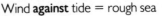

TIDAL STREAM

Wind **with** tide = flat sea

Wind **against** tide = rough sea

*Note*
To clear a narrow passage, or to round a cape, have the wind with the tide. If they are opposed wait for slack water when the sea will be calmer.

## Becalmed
(and no engine)
Prepare to anchor (backing it with a second anchor if there is a strong set).

Get out paddles or scull.
Fix you position.

# —— Tidal Streams ——

## Lateral Counter-Currents

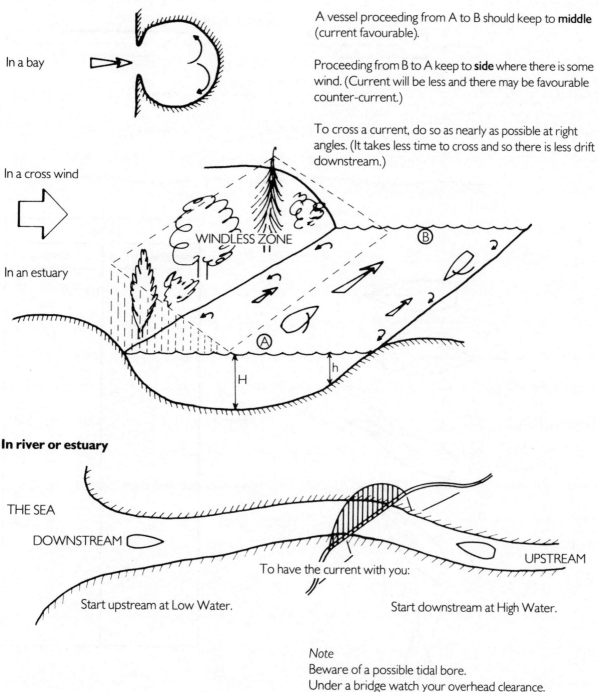

In a bay

In a cross wind

In an estuary

A vessel proceeding from A to B should keep to **middle** (current favourable).

Proceeding from B to A keep to **side** where there is some wind. (Current will be less and there may be favourable counter-current.)

To cross a current, do so as nearly as possible at right angles. (It takes less time to cross and so there is less drift downstream.)

WINDLESS ZONE

B

A

H

h

## In river or estuary

THE SEA

DOWNSTREAM

UPSTREAM

To have the current with you:

Start upstream at Low Water.

Start downstream at High Water.

*Note*
Beware of a possible tidal bore.
Under a bridge watch your overhead clearance.
To avoid running aground look out for shoals at Low
    Water.

# — Tidal Streams—

Heading stream : deduct.
Following stream : add.

Speed of vessel

5 Kt.                                5 Kt.

If you ignore tidal stream, you
Drift off course,
Make little headway, even lose
ground, and may be benighted.

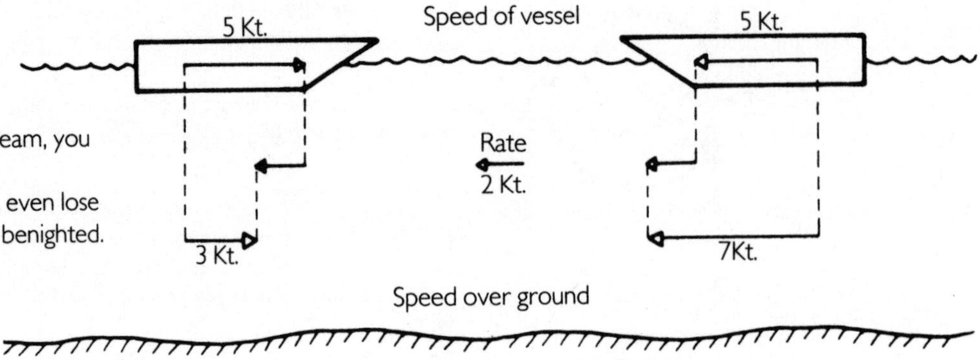

Rate
2 Kt.

3 Kt.                                7Kt.

Speed over ground

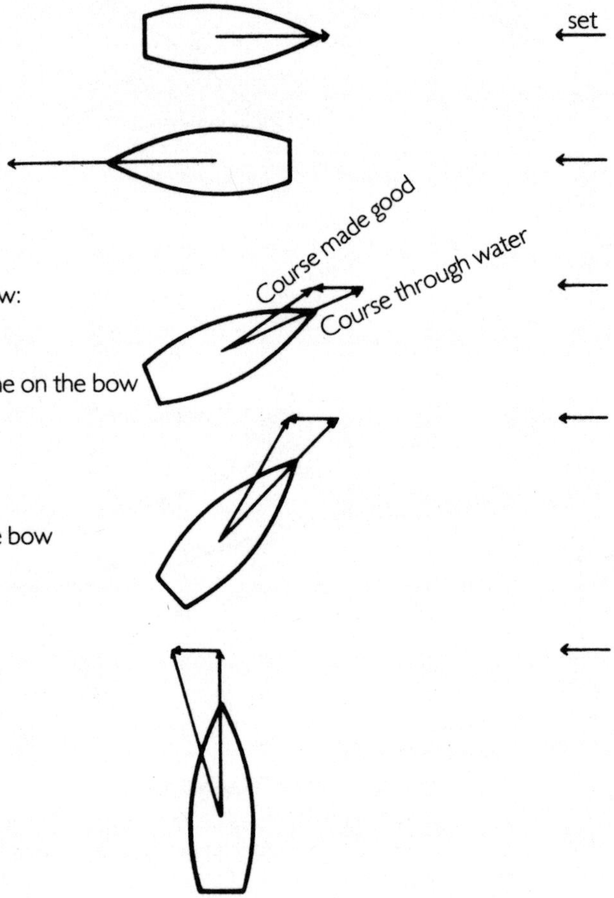

| | The Boat | |
|---|---|---|
| | Speed over ground | Drift |
| Set fore and aft: | | |
| set | Less | Nil |
| | More | Nil |
| Set off the bow: | Less | Little |
| Fine on the bow | | |
| | Somewhat less | Moderate |
| At 45° on the bow | | |
| | Somewhat more | Considerable |
| Abeam | | |

Course made good
Course through water

# ——Drift and Leeway——

Inshore
Due to wind and/or tide

## Sighting ahead

To see if you are drifting to port or starboard.

The helmsman's eye

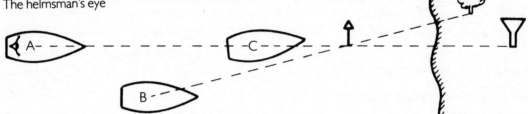

A  We are in line with water tower and beacon, and want to stay that way.

B  Water tower is now to right of beacon.

| The more distant object moves to the right. We are drifting to **starboard**, and vice versa. |
| :-- |
| A drift to starboard is corrected by turning to **port**, and vice versa. |

C  We are back on the line and steering about 5° to port. If we still drift to starboard, we must get back onto the line and steer 8° or 10° to port, etc.

| Close inshore, or in narrows, correct for drift by trial and error. |
| :-- |

## Sighting abeam

To tell if you are making headway or falling back (with the stream).

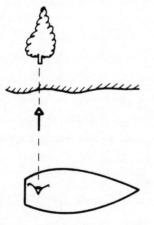

| The more distant mark<br>    Moves **ahead**:  we are stemming the tide.<br>    Moves **astern**:  we are falling back: BEWARE! |
| :-- |

## Various marks:

Pontoon floats, buoys, perches, rock awash, mooring chains, etc., all indicate **direction of stream.**

## Floating objects

Half submerged and not affected by the wind, in relation to a nearby fixed mark, show **rate and set of stream.**

# ——— Leeway ———

Can be measured but is usually estimated.

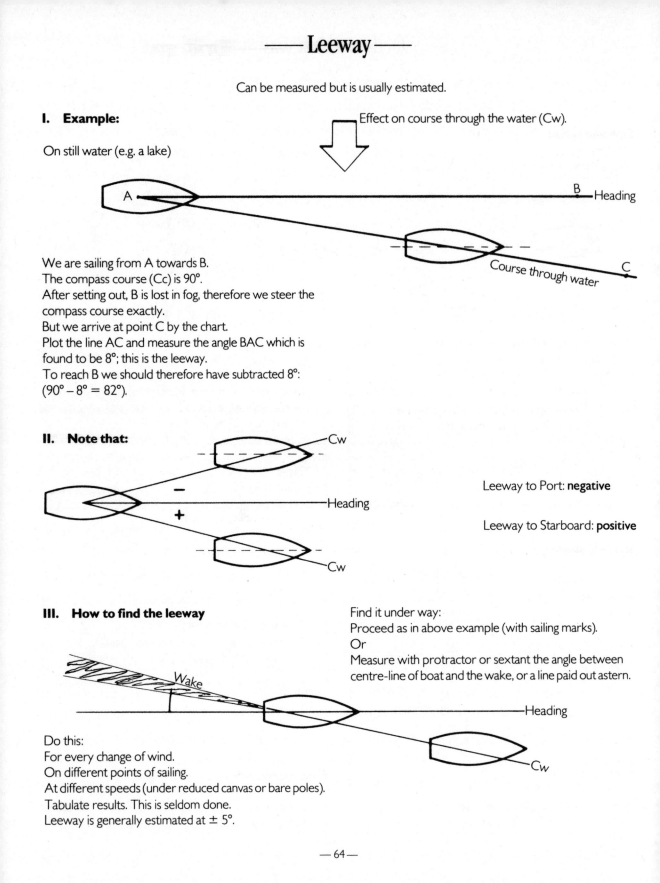

## I. Example:

Effect on course through the water (Cw).

On still water (e.g. a lake)

We are sailing from A towards B.
The compass course (Cc) is 90°.
After setting out, B is lost in fog, therefore we steer the
compass course exactly.
But we arrive at point C by the chart.
Plot the line AC and measure the angle BAC which is
found to be 8°; this is the leeway.
To reach B we should therefore have subtracted 8°:
(90° − 8° = 82°).

## II. Note that:

Leeway to Port: **negative**

Leeway to Starboard: **positive**

## III. How to find the leeway

Find it under way:
Proceed as in above example (with sailing marks).
Or
Measure with protractor or sextant the angle between
centre-line of boat and the wake, or a line paid out astern.

Do this:
For every change of wind.
On different points of sailing.
At different speeds (under reduced canvas or bare poles).
Tabulate results. This is seldom done.
Leeway is generally estimated at ± 5°.

# —— Drift ——

To calculate tidal drift, plot on chart (by reference to True North) the effect on course made good (Cmg). Examples:

## I. No wind, still water

    (e.g. a lake)

A motor vessel proceeds from A towards B.

A ————————————— Speed of vessel ————————————— B

                        Speed over ground

Course through water

Course made good

The compass course is noted and carefully followed.
An hour later the vessel arrives at B, a distance of 5 miles.
One notes that:
   Course through water = Course made good
   Speed over water = Speed over ground (5 kt.)

## II. No wind, on tideway

A motor vessel proceeds from A towards B.

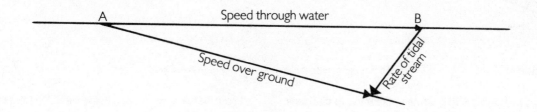

Again:
Compass course carefully followed.
Speed through water 5 kt.

But an hour later boat reaches C, so that C takes the place of B.
**BC represents the rate and set of tidal stream.**
The triangle ABC is the **velocity triangle.**
One notes that: Course through water and Course made good are different.
AC is shorter than AB (in this case) so that speed over ground is less.

*Note*
The tidal stream represents the movement of the whole water mass on which you are sailing. Its characteristics are given in the Sailing Directions, Tide Tables and Charts. On the other hand, with inshore currents and tidal streams, which are like rivers in the sea, one has to discover the drift by trial and error.

# ── Drift ──

On the chart the triangle of velocities gives you the course to steer which is the basis of your reckoning.
　　You have to know, or estimate, the speed of the vessel.

**Two solutions** to reach B, taking account of tidal stream. The rate and direction of the tidal stream are the same from start to finish.

## Solution I

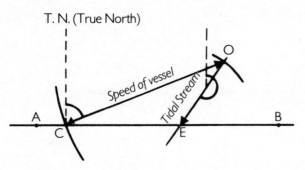

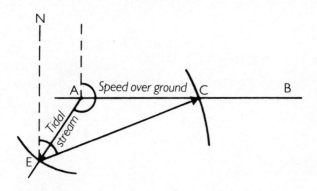

**Alternative (a):** Set off velocity triangle **upstream** from some point on course.
Plot the rate and direction of set **upstream** from AB.
From O (upstream end of set) mark off a distance equal to speed to meet AB at C.
Angle NCO in degrees is the course to steer.
Measure CE for your speed over the ground.

**Alternative (b):** (displacement of point of departure.)
Plot rate and direction of set **downstream** from A.
From the downstream end E mark off a distance equal to speed to meet AB at C.
Angle NEC is course to steer.
AC is your speed over the ground.

## Solution II

a) Passage is from A to B which is expected to take four hours. Direction and rate of tidal stream will vary during passage.
To displace the point of departure:
Draw AB, the intended course.

From A. mark off the successive directions and rates and join A'B.
Angle between A'B and True North is course to steer (Cs).

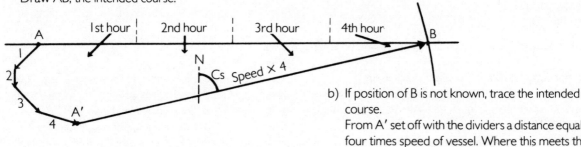

b) If position of B is not known, trace the intended course.
From A' set off with the dividers a distance equal to four times speed of vessel. Where this meets the track will determine point B.

# —— Compass ——
## Variation and Deviation

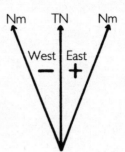

## Variation

Variation (referred to True North) = angle between True North (TN) and North magnetic (Nm), and shown on chart.
Variation to the left (West) is NEGATIVE.
Variation to the right (East) is POSITIVE.

## Deviation

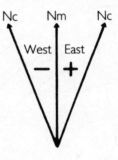

Deviation (referred to Magnetic North) = angle between North magnetic (Nm) and North by the compass (Nc). (It is read off from a deviation curve prepared by you or an expert.)
Deviation to the left (West) is NEGATIVE.
Deviation to the right (East) is POSITIVE.

**Specimen Deviation Curve**

*Example*
For a magnetic heading (Mh) of 90° we allow a deviation of 3° W. (or −3°).
**Compass adjusting** is the procedure of inserting soft iron bars in the binnacle to reduce instrumental error.
**Compass correction** is the preparation of a deviation curve to reduce any residual error.

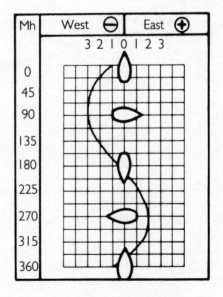

## Compass error

(Ce) is the combined effect of **variation and deviation.**

# ——Compass——

**Angles**

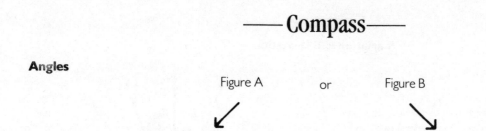

Figure A          or          Figure B

will remind you of the algebraic formulae.

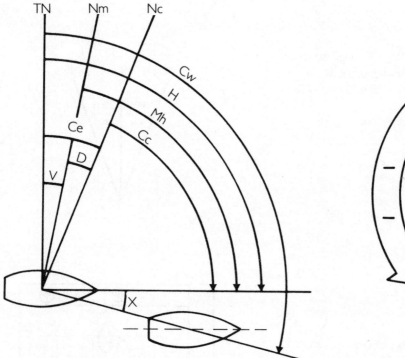

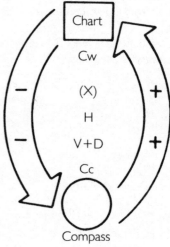

TN    True North (or geographic North)
Nm   North magnetic
Nc    North by compass
Cw   Course through the water
Ce    Compass error: Variation plus Deviation
V      Variation
D      Deviation
H      Heading (referred to True North)
Mh   Magnetic heading (referred to North magnetic)
Cc    Compass course (referred to North by compass)
X      Leeway

*Examples*
From Figs. A or B above:
Cw–X = H
Cc+V+D = H
H+X = Cw
etc.

*Note*
If there is no leeway, Cw = H

# —— Compass ——

**Bearings**

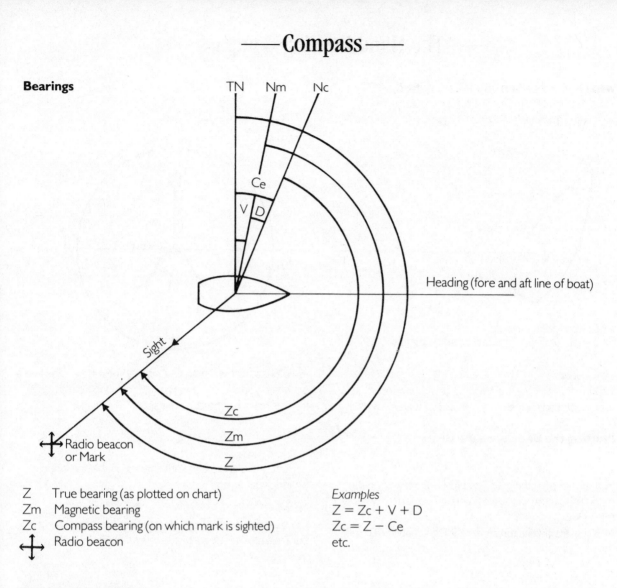

Z    True bearing (as plotted on chart)
Zm   Magnetic bearing
Zc    Compass bearing (on which mark is sighted)
⬦    Radio beacon

*Examples*
$Z = Zc + V + D$
$Zc = Z - Ce$
etc.

## The Direction-Finder
The signal is **weakest** when:

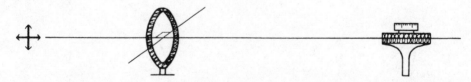

The frame aerial is **perpendicular to station.**     The ferrite is directed **towards station.**

*Note*
An RDF bearing should be treated with reserve:
   At night, and particularly at dusk and dawn (best time = mid-day).
   When line of sight is along-shore or close inshore.

When reading is taken the RDF compass must be kept away from metallic objects and electrical equipment (stays, loud-speakers, metal spectacle frames, etc.).
**Consol** should not be used within 30 miles of the transmitter.

# The Hand Bearing-Compass

## What happens when you take a sight ?

Supposing that the deviation of the hand bearing-compass is zero, so Nc = Nm.

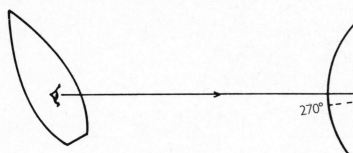

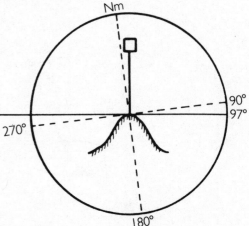

*Example*
Compass reading 97° (Zc), magnetic variation 7° W.

*Explanation*
Imagine that the compass you hold in your hand is superimposed on the mark you are sighting, or on the radio beacon. It will then give you the bearing, i.e. the line on which you are situated running from the boat through the 97° mark on the compass scale.

## Plotting the Bearing on the Chart

This is done by:
Putting a protractor graduated from 0° to 360° on the mark or beacon (with zero pointing True North or along a meridian).
Ruling a straight line through the 90° graduation (97° − 7°).
Then:

$$Z = Zc + V + D$$
$$= 97° + (− 7°)$$
$$= 97° − 7°$$
$$= 90°$$

Boat must have been somewhere on this line when bearing was taken.

*Note*
On board, instead of a protractor and ruler one uses a parallel ruler which combines the functions of both.

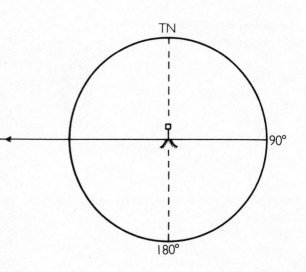

# —— Radio Direction-Finder ——

## Example

A radio beacon on an island or light-vessel out of sight.

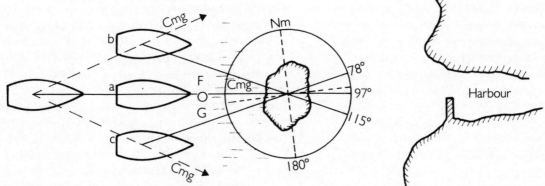

Without changing course (course originally set for island):
if a)  Second bearing same as first: you are on course for island (97°).
 b)  Second bearing greater than first: you will pass to north of island (115°).
 c)  Second bearing less than first: you will pass to south of island (78°).

## Homing

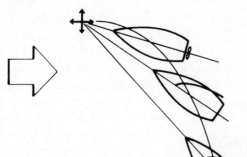

An easy way to steer towards a radio beacon in the absence of chart-table for plotting.

*Principle*
Take D.F. bearings on the beacon and steer on that compass course after each bearing.
Remember that if there is drift or leeway you will get different compass courses if the bearings are taken at regular intervals of 15 or 30 minutes.

*Example*
With steady wind abeam or broad on the bow you will sail in a curve and finish up-wind towards the beacon (under engine). Curve depends on degree of drift.

## Morse code

| | | | | | | | | |
|---|---|---|---|---|---|---|---|---|
| A | .— | J | .——— | S | ... | 2 | ..——— | É | ..—.. |
| B | —... | K | —.— | T | — | 3 | ...—— | Ö | ———. |
| C | —.—. | L | .—.. | U | ..— | 4 | ....— | Ü | ..—— |
| D | —.. | M | —— | V | ...— | 5 | ..... | ñ | ——.—— |
| E | . | N | —. | W | .—— | 6 | —.... | à | .——.— |
| F | ..—. | O | ——— | X | —..— | 7 | ——... | CH | ———— |
| G | ——. | P | .——. | Y | —.—— | 8 | ———.. | Ä | .—.— |
| H | .... | Q | ——.— | Z | ——.. | 9 | ————. | | |
| I | .. | R | .—. | 1 | .———— | 0 | ————— | | |

*Example*
Le Havre (light-vessel).
Identification L.H.( .—.. ....) 291.9 kHz

# ——Course to Steer——

## Graphical Solution

This obviates algebraic calculation and the errors of sign that it may involve, and gives the navigator a quick and realistic appreciation of his whereabouts.

There are three steps:
1. Plot the course made good (Cmg).
2. Find the course through the water (Cw).
3. Calculate the compass course (Cc).

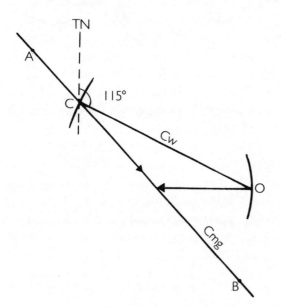

Data:
Passage from A to B.
On passage the tidal stream is 270°, rate of 4 kt.
With wind on port quarter, our estimated speed will be 8 kt.
Leeway will be 2° to starboard.
Magnetic Variation 7° W.
Compass Deviation 3° E.

### On the chart

1. **Plot course made good:** join AB.
2. **Find course through the water.**
   Plot the set and rate of tidal stream (upstream from AB to O).
   Lay off the speed of the boat from O to cut AB at C.
   Measure the angle NCO (115°).
   (If there were no tide Cmg would be the same as Cw.)

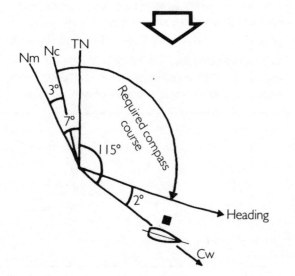

### On a sheet of paper

(In order not to clutter up the chart draw this diagram freehand.) Plot:
   TN.
   Nm (write in the value of V).
   Nc (East means 'to the right'. If there were no deviation Nm would = Nc.)
   Cw
   Heading. (It will be to the left of Cw since the drift is to the right.)
3. **Calculate compass course Cc.**
   We see from the sketch that:
   Cc = 4° + 113° = 117°
   (7° − 3°) + (115° − 2°) = 117°

—72—

# ——Course to Steer——

## Algebraic Solution

Three steps, as before:
1. Plot the course made good (Cmg).
2. Find the course through the water (Cw).
3. Calculate the compass course (Cc).

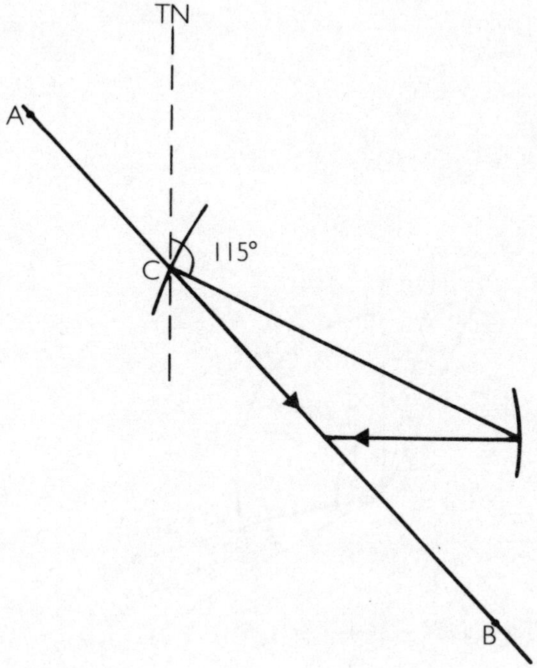

With the same data as on previous page:

### On the chart

1. **Plot Cmg** by joining AB.
2. **Find Cw** as on previous page.

### On a sheet of paper

3. **Calculate Cc.**
   From the diagrams on p.68:
   $$Cc = Cw - X - (V+D)$$
   $$= 115° - (+2°) - [(-7°) + (+3°)]$$
   $$= 115° - (+2°) - (-7° + 3°)$$
   $$= 115° - 2° + 7° - 3°$$
   $$= 122° - 5°$$
   $$= 117°$$

# ── The Compass Course ──

To determine the true course made good (Cmg) from the
compass course steered.
    Two steps:
1. Find the course through the water (Cw).
2. Plot the course made good (Cmg).

*Data*
Helmsman has steered a compass course of 117°.
Magnetic Variation = 7° W.
Compass Deviation = 3° E.
Wind on port quarter and estimated leeway of 2° to
starboard.
Speedometer reads 8 kt.
Tidal stream is 270° and the rate 4 kt.

## I. On a sheet of paper

Find the course through the water Cw.

**(a) By freehand diagram:**
Draw TN, Nm, Nc, Cc and Cw, or

**(b) By algebra** (see page 68):
$$
\begin{aligned}
Cw &= Cc + V + D + X \\
   &= 117° + (-7°) + (+3°) + (+2°) \\
   &= 117° - 7° + 3° + 2° \\
   &= 122° - 7° \\
   &= 115°
\end{aligned}
$$

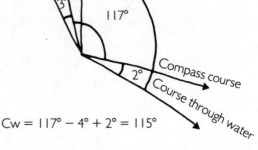

$Cw = 117° - 4° + 2° = 115°$

## II. On the chart

Plot the course made good.
From D (the last fix on the chart)
Plot Cw (115°)
Plot DO (= 8 kt)
From O draw OE (= 4 kt)
Join DE
Length DE is the speed over the ground.

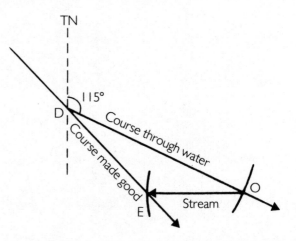

# The Log Book

The official record which is evidence in the event of an accident.
Essential for your dead reckoning.
*Must* be kept up if there is risk of fog.

## Specimen

| Time | Compass course | Mean Speedometer reading (kt) | Log (miles) | Echo Sounder (metres) | Barometer (mb.) | Wind (dir.) | Wind (force) | Estimated leeway | Remarks |
|------|---------------|-------------------------------|-------------|-----------------------|-----------------|-------------|--------------|------------------|---------|
| 1200 | 060° | 6 | 428 | | 1000 | NW | 4 | 3° Stbd. | |
| 1300 | 080° | 5 | 434 | 30 | 1000 | NW | 3 | 2° Stbd. | Fog |
| 1400 | | | | | | | | | |
| 1500 | 250° | 8 | 445 | 21 | 998 | W | 6 | 5° Port | |
| 1600 | | | | 17 | | | | | |
| 1700 | | 4 | 462 | 20 | | W | 3 | | |
| 1800 | 140° | 4 | 466 | 18 | 999 | W | 3 | Nil | |
| 1830 | 150° | 3 | 468 | 10 | 1000 | W | 2 | | |

We know that in this area V = 6° W.
D = Nil

*Note*
A N.W. wind blows **from** the north-west.

# —— Dead Reckoning ——

Required in darkness or fog.
Required in absence of radio aids.
What you must have:
    Log book
    Local chart.

## Algebraic Solution

### I.  On a sheet of paper

Find course through the water, (see LOG BOOK on
preceding page).

Specimen table

| Time | Course through water (Cc + V + D + X) | Distance covered (n.m.) |
|---|---|---|
| 1200 | | |
| | $060° + (-6°) + (+3°)$ <br> $060° - 6° + 3° = 057°$ | 6 |
| 1300 | | |
| | $080° + (-6°) + (+2°)$ <br> $080° - 6° + 2° = 076°$ | 11 |
| 1500 | | |
| | $250° + (-6°) + (-5°)$ <br> $250° - 6° - 5° = 239°$ | 21 |
| 1800 | | |
| | $140° + (-6°)$ <br> $140° - 6°\qquad = 134°$ | 2 |
| 1830 | | |

## II.  On the chart

a) **Plot Cw** from the last fix, D.
b) **Plot tidal streams** to find your true position on chart
   and displacement of your chart position from surface
   track (A).

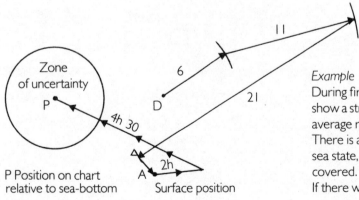

P Position on chart
relative to sea-bottom

Surface position

*Example*
During first two hours of passage, tidal insets on chart
show a stream of 085° and a rate of 2 kt., then 295° and an
average rate of 3 kt.
There is always some degree of uncertainty (helmsman,
sea state, etc.) equivalent to some 10 per cent of distance
covered.
If there were no tide, A would be the required position.

# —— Dead Reckoning ——

## Graphical Solution

### I. On a sheet of paper

Make a freehand sketch for each compass course steered
(Cc) in order to find the course through the water (Cw).

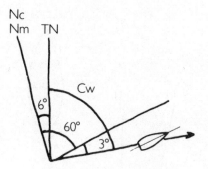

a) on course 060°
   Plot:
   TN
   Nm
   Nc (the same as Nm, as D = 0)
   Cc
   Leeway (to starboard as the wind is NW.)
   Then: Cw = 60° − 6° + 3° = 057°
   Distance by log = 434 − 428 = 6 n.m.

b) on course 080°: Cw = 076°
   Distance = 445 − 434 = 11 n.m.

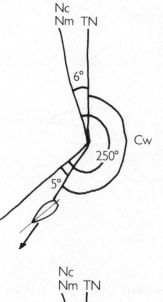

c) on course 250°:
   Here leeway is to port as wind is W.
   Cw = 250° − 6° − 5° = 239°
   Distance by log = 466 − 445 = 21 n.m.

d) on course 140°
   No leeway: Cw = H
   Cw = 140° − 6° = 134°
   Distance by log = 468 − 466 = 2 n.m.

*Note*
You can easily draw these four diagrams in fifteen minutes.

### II. On the chart

a) **Plot the corrected courses (Cw).**
b) **Plot the drifts** (as on preceding page).

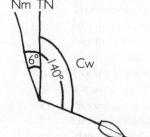

# —— Transits ——

You can fix your position from:

Two TRANSITS (exact)

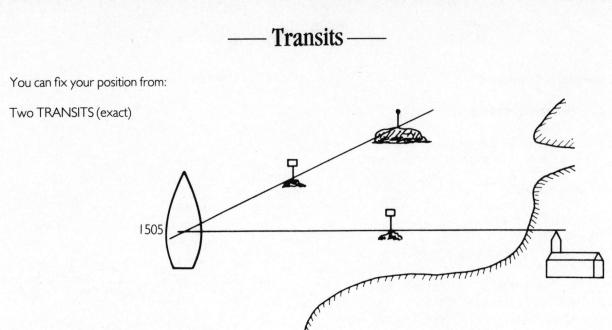

1505

Always note time of fix.

A TRANSIT and a MARK (fairly accurate)

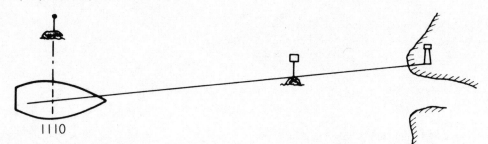

1110

Lighthouse is in line with can buoy.
Mark is abeam.

A TRANSIT and a SOUNDING (useful)

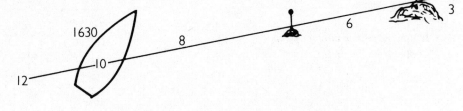

15

1630

12

10

8

6

3

*Example*
Sounding shows 12 metres.
Time, 1630, Height of tide = 2 m.
Therefore look for a depth of (12 − 2 = 10) m. on the chart.

For safety, a transit should be on two well separated fixed marks.
Tidal streams and currents affect the position of a buoy.
Use a transit to check compass or find deviation.

# —— Bearings ——

You can fix your position from:

A TRANSIT and a BEARING, to a mark or to a radio beacon (fairly accurate)

With the hand bearing-compass a lighthouse bears 160°.
(Variation = − 7°)
On account of motion in small boats you might be out by about 5° (155° or 165°); there is therefore a SECTOR OF UNCERTAINTY.

Always note time of fix.

Two or three BEARINGS to marks or radio beacons (useful)

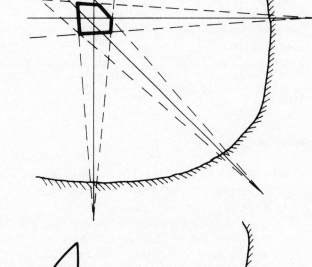

The first two bearings should be as nearly as possible at right angles.
The third bearing allows you to
Check the other two, and
Reduce area of uncertainty.

A BEARING and a SOUNDING (useful)

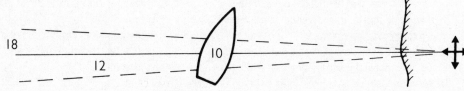

# —— Coastal Navigation ——

Avoid unfavourable weather conditions and the sun in your eyes.

## Requisites

Knowing your tides
A watch
The chart

## Method

Navigation in an area of off-lying rocks calls for **constant vigilance.** A very sensible way of reading the chart is to attach it to a light board half as wide as the chart itself. When using the chart on deck always orient it correctly (with North on the chart towards True North) so that you will pick up landmarks in the order in which they are shown on the chart.

## Identification of rocks

As seen from on board there appears to be a passage between 9 and 12.

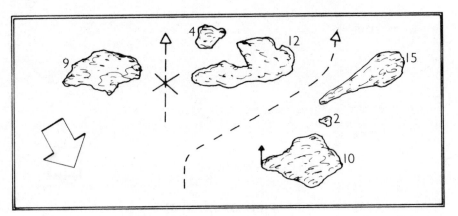

From the chart, however, this is to be avoided: Too close on wind for 4.

However between 12 and 15 is possible.

## Remarks

Mark direction of apparent wind on your chart and choose courses between sailing free and a broad reach (a cross current may oblige you to go close hauled).

Watch tidal streams (strongest at mid-tide). A beginner should wait for the slack at High or Low Water.

On a running course speed of boat must be sufficient for you to stem tide if necessary.

Rocks close by are darker than those at mid-distance.

A high rock may take the wind out of your sails.

Remember that you may be able to check your tidal calculations against rocks awash, or even tide gauge.

When threading your way through many hazards make a habit of tracing your track, freehand, on the chart as you go along.

If you are unable to identify a rock, or a group of rocks, drop anchor.

Around Low Water there are more rocks uncovered; this makes identification easier and it is therefore safer to go through.

# — Approaches —

The apparent wind is the principal factor in choosing the
route; avoid approaching up-wind if possible.

## With one or two transits to avoid dangers
### (exact)

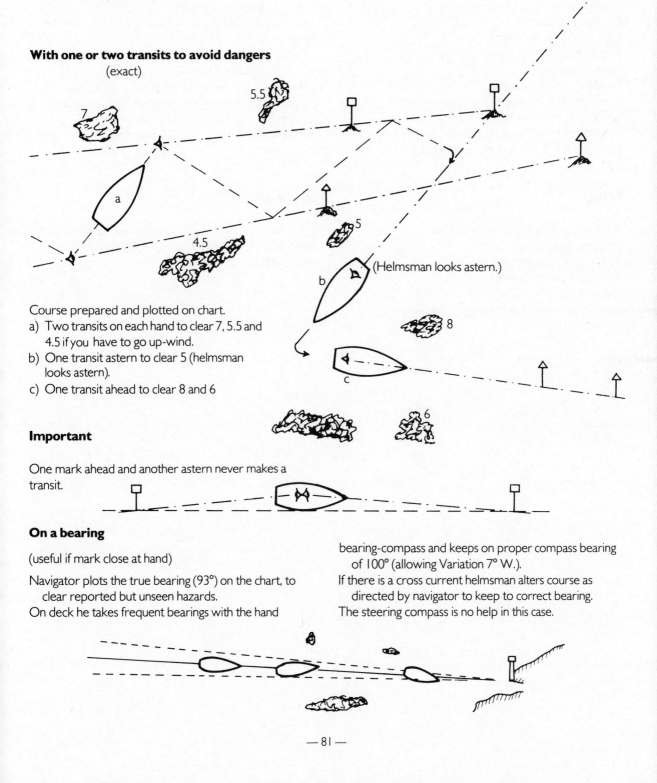

Course prepared and plotted on chart.
a) Two transits on each hand to clear 7, 5.5 and
   4.5 if you have to go up-wind.
b) One transit astern to clear 5 (helmsman
   looks astern).
c) One transit ahead to clear 8 and 6

(Helmsman looks astern.)

## Important

One mark ahead and another astern never makes a
transit.

## On a bearing

(useful if mark close at hand)

Navigator plots the true bearing (93°) on the chart, to
   clear reported but unseen hazards.
On deck he takes frequent bearings with the hand
bearing-compass and keeps on proper compass bearing
   of 100° (allowing Variation 7° W.).
If there is a cross current helmsman alters course as
   directed by navigator to keep to correct bearing.
The steering compass is no help in this case.

# —— Fog ——

## When fog is expected

Reduce sail to moderate proportions (no spinnaker).
Fix your position.
Decide on an exact course.
Work out tides for the area.
Keep an exact log.
Get your fog-horn ready.
Listen to weather forecast if possible.
See that all iron objects are in their right places.
Inshore, if you have no echo-sounder, get the lead and line
    ready and be prepared to cast anchor.

## In fog

Wear your life-jacket (in case of collision).
a) **Steer** by compass.
b) Fix your **position:**
        by dead reckoning.
and/or  by D. F.
        by soundings (and depth contours on chart).

c) If you are **approaching land:**
        Proceed from buoy to buoy.
        Steer by compass.
and/or  Use D. F. (unless you are too close).
        Take soundings.
        Carry your sounding forward on chart.
        Interpolate between soundings.
(The last two are easier to work out at the High or Low
Water Stand, when there is generally little or no tidal
stream.)
d) **Open sea:** Head for open water if making shore too
    complicated.

## Becalmed

If you anchor, do so in shallow water (out of the way of
deep-draught vessels and possible collision).
Avoid grounding (p.114)

# —— Fog Signals ——
## (by day or night)

A long blast from 4 to 6 seconds.
A short blast about one second.

| Type of ship | Nature of signal | | | |
|---|---|---|---|---|
| | Device | Signal | | Frequency |
| Power-driven vessel under way | Siren or Whistle | One prolonged blast | — | 2 min. |
| Power-driven vessel not making way through water | Siren or Whistle | Two prolonged blasts separated by interval of two seconds | — — | 2 min. |
| Vessel at anchor; under 100 m. in length | Bell | Rings the bell rapidly for 5 seconds | | 1 min. |
| Over 100 m. | Bell and Gong | Rings the bell for'ard and then beats gong aft | | 1 min. |
| All vessels at anchor | Siren, Whistle or Foghorn | May also sound three blasts in succession, short, long, short | · — · | 1 min. |
| Vessel aground | Siren, Whistle (or Foghorn) and Bell | Signal for vessel at anchor plus three distinct strokes on bell before and after signal | | 1 min. |
| Sailing vessel, vessel engaged in towing, laying buoys etc. or not under control | Siren or Whistle (Foghorn if under sail) | A long blast followed by two short blasts | — · · | 2 min. |
| Vessel under tow, or last of such vessels if more than one | Siren, Whistle or Foghorn | Immediately after the signal from the towing vessel, a long blast followed by three short blasts | — · · · | 2 min. |

Do not confuse these signals with the manoeuvring signals when vessels are in sight of one another.

1 short blast: I am altering course to starboard.
2 short blasts: I am altering course to port.
3 short blasts: My engines are going in reverse.

5 short blasts: (to attract attention).
At a distance it is not easy to judge the direction of a signal but a tube held to the ear (rolled up chart for example) will be a great help.

# ——Depth Contours——

With a favourable wind it is useful and quite easy to follow a depth contour.

## What you require

Knowledge of your approximate position (circle of error).
Knowledge of state of tide.
Local chart.
Reliable echo-sounder (or lead and line).

## Example

To enter a harbour.

Wind due West.

Beacon on 5-metre contour.

Tower beacon on 10-metre contour.

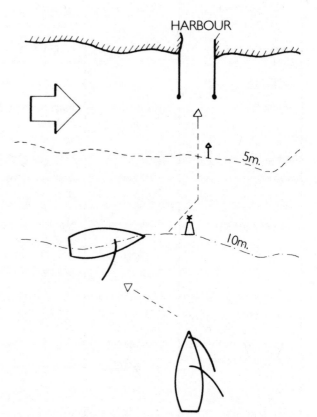

## Method

Steer well upwind of tower beacon.
Take sounding and reduce it, as follows:

| | |
|---|---|
| At a given time the sounding is | 22 m. |
| Calculated height of tide is | 8 m. |
| Charted depth is | 14 m. |

If you see a lobster-pot, note rate and set of any tidal stream.

When you reach the 10-metre contour turn down wind and then take in jib (to reduce speed and for better visibility).
When you reach the tower beacon steer for other beacon and then harbour entrance. Hoist jib again.

*Note*
If your reckoning brings you to the 10-metre contour down wind from the tower you will have to beat to windward to get back to it.

If there are hazards to navigation outside the fairway, or a cross current, and you cannot see the entrance, it is better to hold off and look for a good anchorage.

# ——— Carrying Forward a Depth Contour ———

*What you require:*
Knowledge of your approximate position (circle of error).
Knowledge of state of tide.
Large-scale chart with plenty of contours.
Echo-sounder.
Log.

**I.  With two contours**

1. Fix your position (and draw circle of error).
2. Calculate course made good. Draw parallel tangents to circle of error and mark points A and B where they cut the 30-metre contour.
   Calculate speed over ground.
       When you reach 30-metre contour:
3. Note time ($T_1$). (You are now on AB.)
   Read log.
4. Put a piece of squared tracing paper over chart (with the squares in line with the meridians and parallels).

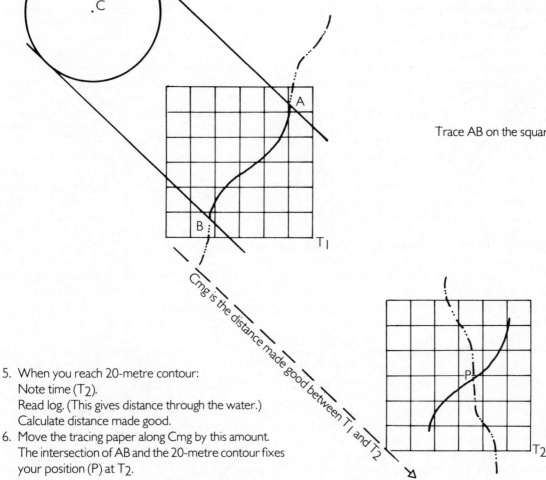

Trace AB on the squared paper.

5. When you reach 20-metre contour:
   Note time ($T_2$).
   Read log. (This gives distance through the water.)
   Calculate distance made good.
6. Move the tracing paper along Cmg by this amount.
   The intersection of AB and the 20-metre contour fixes your position (P) at $T_2$.

*Note*
The log reading can be used if speed over ground has not been worked out.

## II.  With three contours

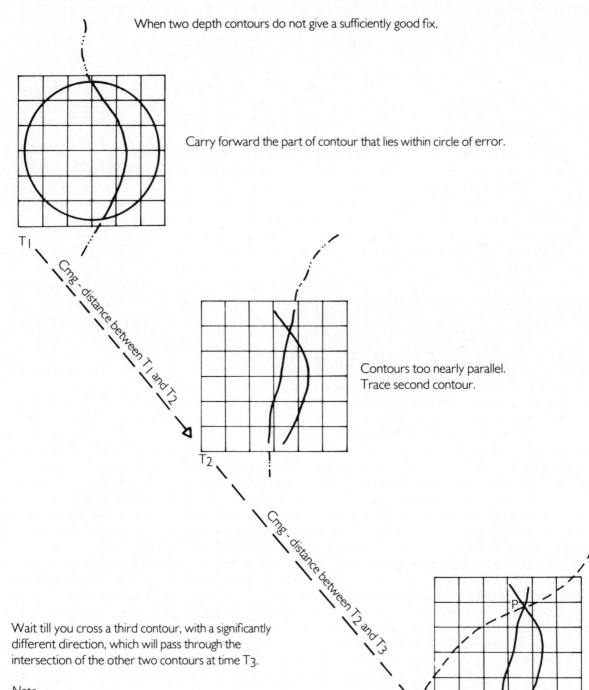

When two depth contours do not give a sufficiently good fix.

Carry forward the part of contour that lies within circle of error.

T₁

Cmg - distance between T₁ and T₂

Contours too nearly parallel.
Trace second contour.

T₂

Cmg - distance between T₂ and T₃

Wait till you cross a third contour, with a significantly
different direction, which will pass through the
intersection of the other two contours at time T₃.

P

*Note*
You may have to alter course to cross a suitable third
contour.

T₃

# —— Interpolation of Soundings ——

Particularly useful if bottom is irregular or if there are no depth contours on chart.

## I. On a sheet of squared tracing paper

Plot (at chart scale):
    Course through water, Cw  (in one hour).
    Tidal stream               (set and rate).
    Course made good, Cmg   (by joining AC).
This is the velocity triangle.

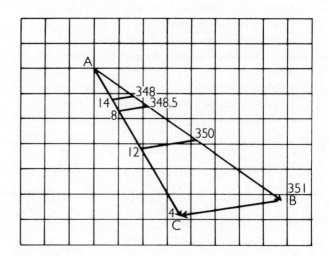

At each round figure on echo-sounder (or at regular intervals with lead and line), record:
    Sounding.
    Time.
    Log reading.

Plot the log readings along line AB. Through these points draw lines parallel to BC to cut line AC.
    At these cuts write down the soundings, **after** deducting height of tide. (After one hour you are at point C.)
From C, the end of Cmg,
Plot:
    New Cw.
    Tidal stream.
    New Cmg.
This gives you a new velocity triangle.
Do not go more than 3 or 4 miles on each leg, in order to limit circle of error.

## II. On the chart

Move the tracing paper parallel to the meridian, bringing point A within circle of error and making the soundings coincide with those on chart.
The course made good as plotted on the tracing paper is now required course on the chart.

# —— Reducing the Circle of Error ——

By successive alterations of course.

## Principle

Leave one depth contour almost at a tangent and cross next one almost at right angles.
1. Find your position P by dead reckoning.
2. Plot course made good up to 30-metre contour on chart.
   Draw circle of error.
   Plot a new course from A and B to the 20-metre contour and work out required course to steer.

3. When you are over the 30-metre contour you may be at A or B or at some point between (limit of error). Alter to new compass course.
   As always, note time and read log.
4. When you reach the 20-metre contour, plot a new course to the 10-metre contour as before and work out course to steer.

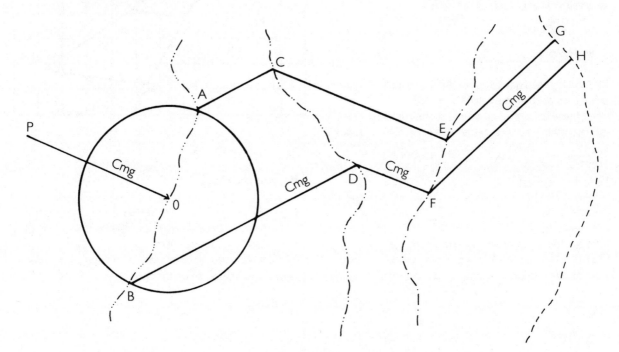

# —— Running Fixes ——

## Successive bearings on a radio beacon

1. Take a D.F. bearing on the beacon.

   **Note:**
   > Compass bearing (Zc).
   > Log reading.
   > Time (1000).

2. Set a course that makes an angle of from 70° to 90°
   with bearing and note this heading.

   $Z$

   70° to 90°       Cmg

   $T_1$

3. **Plot** on the chart:
   > True bearing of beacon (Z).
   > Course made good (see p.74) from $T_1$ (a point
   > somewhere on the plotted true bearing).

4. Take another bearing on the beacon after 15, 30 or 60
   minutes (at not too small an angle with first).
   **Note:**
   > Compass bearing (Zc).
   > Log reading.
   > Time (1030).

   $Z$

   $P$

   $T_2$       $T_2$

   $P$

5. **Plot** the new true bearing (Z).
   > Distance made good fixes point $T_2$.
   > From $T_2$ draw a line parallel to first bearing to cut
   > second bearing at P (1030).

*Note*
P will be to left or right of Cmg according to the distance
made good.

## Successive bearings on a mark

Two bearings at known times.

## Example

At 1100
**Note:**
    Compass bearing (Zc).
    Log reading.
    Compass course (Cc).
    Time.
**Plot** (on chart):
    True bearing Z (a).
    Course made good (along b).

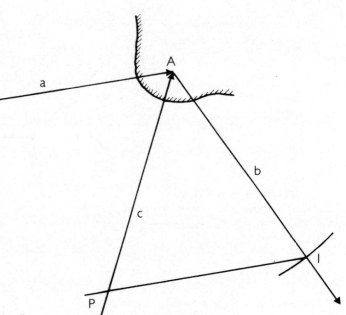

At 1130
**Note:**
    Compass bearing.
    Log reading.
    Compass course.
    Time.
**Plot:**
    True bearing (c).
    Mark off along (b) the distance made good.
    From this point (1) draw line parallel to (a), to cut (c) at P.
    This is your position at 1130.

## Successive bearings on a mark

Doubling the angle on the bow, the first angle being the angle between the true bearing and the Course made good.

I. At 1100:
1. **Note:**
    Compass bearing of mark A.
    Log reading.
    Compass course.
    Time.
2. **Calculate** Course made good as on p. 74.
3. **Plot** on the chart:
    True bearing of A (a).
    Course made good (b) (somewhere near A).
    Measure angle ABR.
    Draw line (c) from A making an angle with (b) that is double the angle ABR.
4. **Note** true bearing of A along line (c).

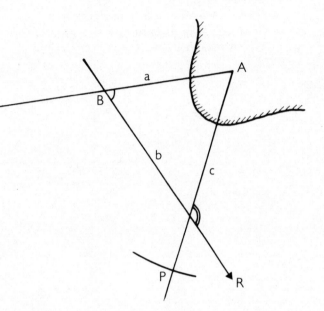

II. With hand bearing-compass, follow bearing of A until it reaches compass bearing corresponding to (c).
   At the moment:
      **Read** the log.
      **Note** the time (1200).
      **Mark off** from A along (c) the distance made good.
   This gives you point P, which is your position at 1200.

## Successive bearings on a mark

The 'Four-point fix' using angles of 45° and 90° between
true bearing and Course made good.

I. Preparation:
   **Plot** on the chart:
      Course made good (a), fairly near point A.
      From A draw line (b) to cut (a) at an angle of 45°.
      From A draw another line (c) to cut (a) at an angle of
      90°.

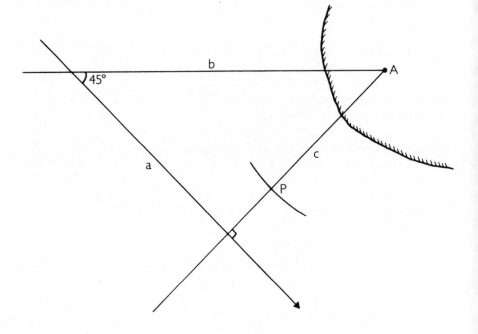

**Note:**
      True bearing of A along line (b).
      True bearing of A along line (c).

II. **Take bearings** on A with hand bearing-compass.
      Wait till you have the calculated compass bearing
      corresponding to (b), then read log and note time
      (0800).
      Now wait till compass bearing corresponds to (c);
      again read log and note time (0925).

III. From A **mark off** a distance along (c) equal to the
      distance made good between the two times. This gives
      you point P, which is your fix at 0925.

# ——— Running Fixes ———

## Successive bearings on two marks

I. At 0900 you sight a mark (A).
   **Note:**
       Compass bearing.
       Log reading.
       Compass course.
       Time (0900).

   **Plot:**
   True bearing (a).

   Mark A is now lost in fog.
   Work out your Course made good (see p. 74).

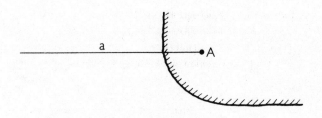

II. At 1100 fog lifts and you sight another mark (B).
   **Note:**
       Compass bearing.
       Log reading.
       Time (1100).

   **Plot:**
       From B, the true bearing (b).
       From A, the Course made good (c) in two hours.
       This fixes point C, through which you draw line (d)
       parallel to (a) and cutting (b) at point P.
       This is your position at 1100.
   (A line through P and parallel to (c) will cut (a) at your
   position at 0900.)

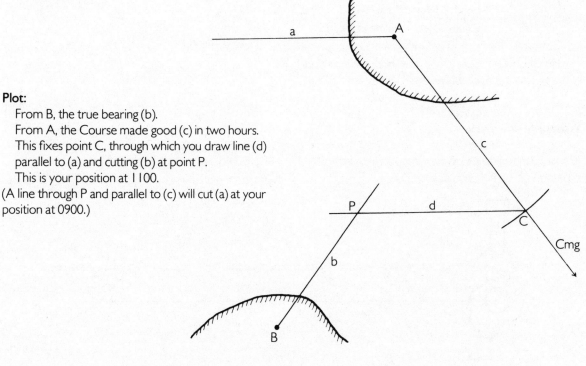

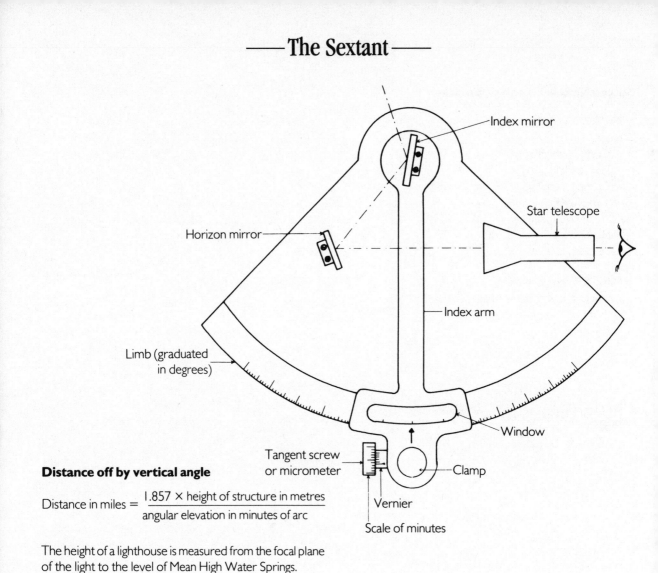

## Distance off by vertical angle

$$\text{Distance in miles} = \frac{1.857 \times \text{height of structure in metres}}{\text{angular elevation in minutes of arc}}$$

The height of a lighthouse is measured from the focal plane of the light to the level of Mean High Water Springs.

## With only one mark

A bearing plus distance off by vertical angle fixes your position.

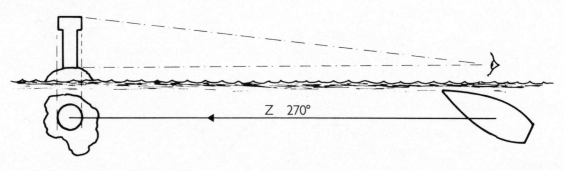

# ——The Sextant——

## One bearing and the horizontal sextant angle between two marks

(a useful method)

1. Plot the true bearing (344°).
2. **Add** the measured angle (100°) to the bearing (*if* B is to right of A) and plot it from B.

   *Example*
   344° + 100° = 444°
   $\qquad\qquad$ = 360° + 84°
   $\qquad\qquad\qquad$ (or 84°)

   > *Note*
   > Always record time of fix.

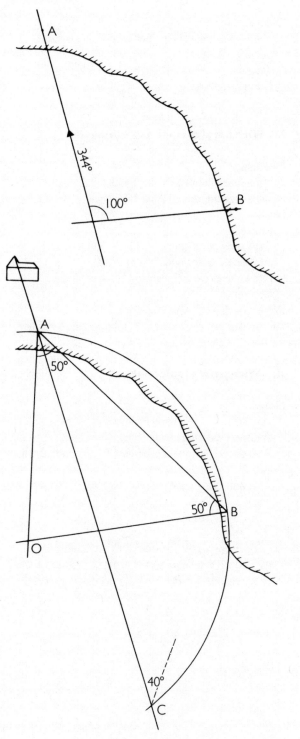

## A transit and the horizontal angle between two marks

(precise)

1. Plot the transit.
2. Plot AB.
3. (90° minus measured angle, which is 40° = 50°).
   Draw lines from A and B making angles of 50° with the line AB. They cut at O.
4. Draw circle through A with centre O to cut the transit at C; which is your required position.

   > *Note*
   > If the measured angle were 90° the centre of the circle would be at mid point of AB.
   > If the measured angle were greater than 90°, for example 110°, the angle (110° − 90° = 20°) would be drawn on the landward side of the line AB.

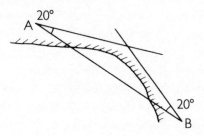

# —— The Sextant ——

## Horizontal angles to three marks

**Record:**
   The two sextant angles, between A and B and
   between B and C.
   Time
   Compass course.

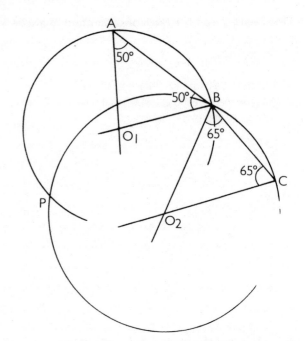

## I.   With parallel ruler and compasses

**Example:**
AB (the first sextant angle $M_1$) = 40°.
BC (the second sextant angle $M_2$) = 25°.
**Draw:**
   Line AB.
   At A draw an angle 90° − $M_1$ = 50°.
   At B draw an angle 90° − $M_1$ = 50°.
   Draw the circle with centre $O_1$ where these lines
   intersect.
Repeat on line BC with angle $M_2$.
Where the two circles cut at P is the required position.

## II.   With parallel ruler only

**Draw:**
   Line AB.
   A perpendicular at A.
   At B draw a line making angle 90° − $M_1$ with the line
   AB.
   At B also draw a line making angle 90° − $M_2$ with the
   line BC.
   Draw a perpendicular at C.
   Join $D_1$ $D_2$
   Drop a perpendicular from B to the line $D_1$ $D_2$
   (produced if necessary). Where it cuts $D_1$ $D_2$ is the
   required position P.

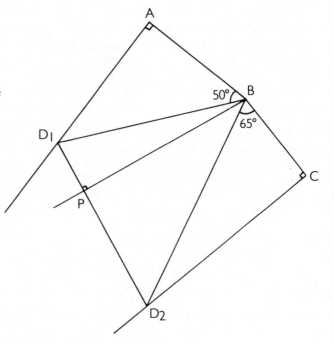

# —— Sailing at Night ——

Navigation is simpler. But distance-judgement is difficult. Rely on your instruments and on external aids.

## I.   Navigation from point to point

Keep on course with steering compass.
Or simply head for a fixed light.

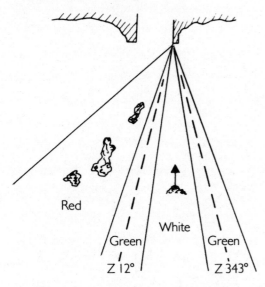

Red

White

Green
Z 12°

Green
Z 343°

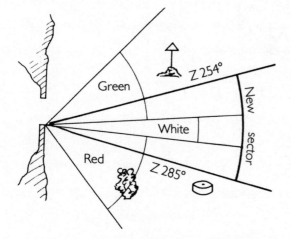

Green

Z 254°

White

New sector

Red

Z 285°

## II.   Making the land with light sectors

The light sectors of a lighthouse are shown as bearings. To make the approach you follow the sector, or sectors, recommended.

*Note*
Some lights with several sectors sometimes have two sectors of the same colour. How do you know which one you are in ?

You see a green light; so you are in one of the green sectors.

Put a parallel ruler along the middle of each of the green sectors, note true bearing (Z) and work out compass bearing (Zc).
(If Variation is 7°W.) Zc = 343° + 7° = 350°
Zc =  12° + 7° = 19°

With hand bearing-compass take a bearing on the light; the nearer value of Zc to the compass bearing shows which sector you are in.

## III.   Making the land where there is a narrow sector

(Not practicable when beating to windward.)

Plot on chart a wider sector that excludes all unlighted hazards (rocks, beacons, buoys, etc. ), but not too close to them.

You have worked out your tides and made sure that the new sector is safe for navigation.
Within this sector you steer entirely by hand bearing-compass. If Variation is 7°W. you must keep inside the bearing limits (Zc) of 261° and 292°.

## IV.   Making the land where the light shows no sectors

Follow same procedure as above.

*Note*
Always refer to the *List of Lights*.

# —— Collision Regulations ——

The INTERNATIONAL REGULATIONS FOR PREVENTING COLLISIONS AT SEA apply to all vessels. New regulations came into force in 1977, mainly to provide for safer navigation with radar and in the one-way traffic lanes of *Separation Schemes*.

You must know the rules and how to apply them when there is a risk of collision.

There is a *Risk of Collision* if the *compass* bearing of an approaching vessel does not change appreciably. Take frequent bearings to make sure it is changing.

When you alter course to avoid risk of collision the change should be large enough to be easily seen by another vessel. Avoid a lot of small alterations, they only confuse others.

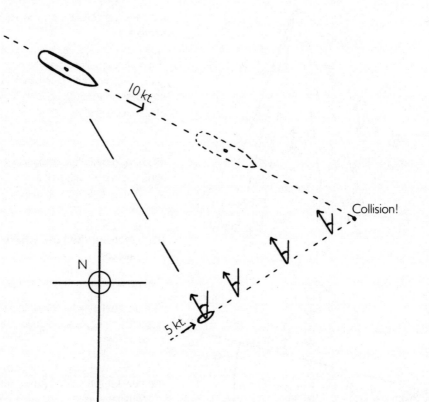

# ⸺ Collision Regulations ⸺

*Vessels in sight of each other*
Here are some of the rules:

1. Keep out of the way of a vessel you are overtaking.
2. Turn to starboard to avoid risk of collision with an approaching vessel.
3. Give way to a vessel crossing ahead of you from starboard to port.
4. If you are not the one to give way do not (if possible) alter course or speed.
5. A power-driven vessel *should* give way to a sailing vessel. (But this may be impossible for a large ship, so get out of the way in good time if you can. Under the new rules a sailing vessel must not impede a power-driven vessel in a traffic lane.)
6. To avoid risk of collision between two sailing vessels the steering rules are simple:

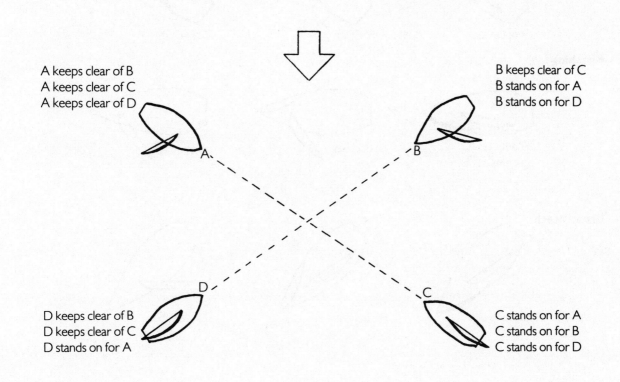

A keeps clear of B
A keeps clear of C
A keeps clear of D

B keeps clear of C
B stands on for A
B stands on for D

D keeps clear of B
D keeps clear of C
D stands on for A

C stands on for A
C stands on for B
C stands on for D

*Note*
Get to know the characteristic lights and shapes displayed by ships of different types.

Do not forget your own navigation lights.
(For sailing in reduced visibility see p. 83.)

# —To Reduce Speed Quickly—

(without altering course)

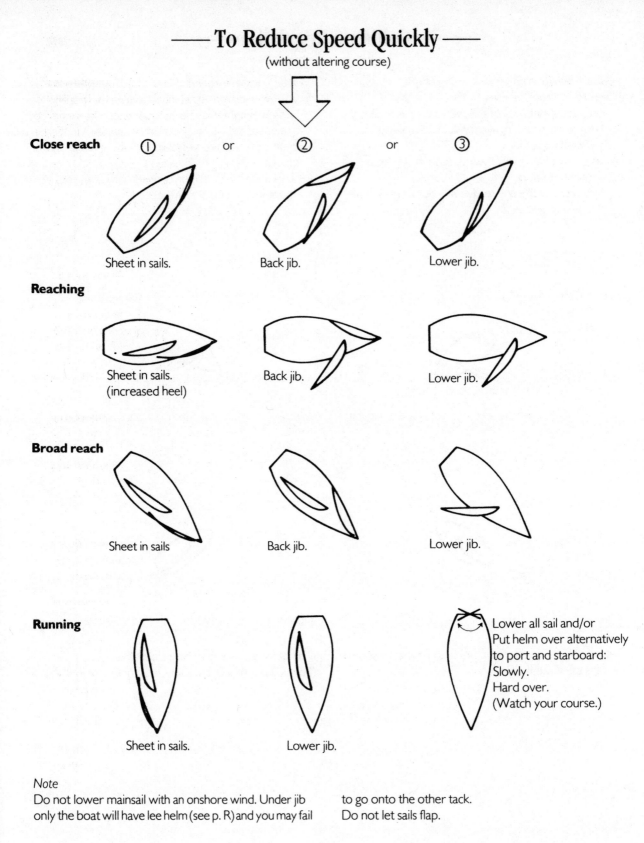

**Close reach**

① or ② or ③

Sheet in sails.

Back jib.

Lower jib.

**Reaching**

Sheet in sails.
(increased heel)

Back jib.

Lower jib.

**Broad reach**

Sheet in sails

Back jib.

Lower jib.

**Running**

Sheet in sails.

Lower jib.

Lower all sail and/or
Put helm over alternatively
to port and starboard:
Slowly.
Hard over.
(Watch your course.)

*Note*
Do not lower mainsail with an onshore wind. Under jib only the boat will have lee helm (see p. R) and you may fail to go onto the other tack.
Do not let sails flap.

# ── Reducing Sail ──

This will depend on boat, sea state, crew, and experience of the skipper.

Briefly: Excessive heel and/or boat heavy on helm = Too much sail or badly balanced sail (p. R).

## Sloop

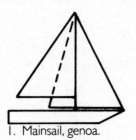

1. Mainsail, genoa.

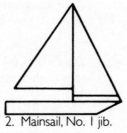

2. Mainsail, No. 1 jib.

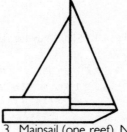

3. Mainsail (one reef), No. 1 or No. 2 jib. (Or often the heavy genoa, one reef.)

*Note*
With moderate wind and heavy sea, choose jib with high foot to be clear of seas breaking over bow.

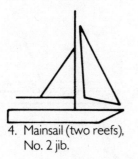

4. Mainsail (two reefs), No. 2 jib.

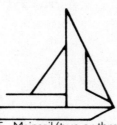

5. Mainsail (two or three reefs), storm jib.

## Ketch

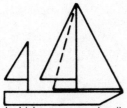

1. Light genoa, mainsail, mizzen.

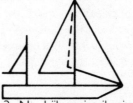

2. Heavy genoa, mainsail, mizzen.

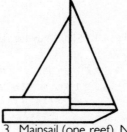

3. No. 1 jib, mainsail, mizzen (one reef).

4. No. 1 jib, mainsail (one reef), mizzen (two reefs).

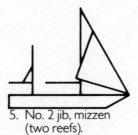

5. No. 2 jib, mizzen (two reefs).

6. Storm jib, mainsail (fully reefed down).

# —— Reefing ——

## When to reef:
Excessive heel.
Squall expected.
Excessive weather helm (boat hard to keep on course).
Crew needs resting.

*Note*
In a strong blow and if you have little experience of reefing, heave-to (p. V) or lower jib.
The hollow of a mainsail (p. M) can be reduced by closing seam at the foot, or replacing it with a flatter sail.

## I.   Turn to windward

Sheet in mainsail amidships.

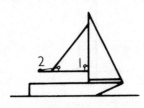

Make sure you have enough sea room to leeward.
1. The helmsman: either secures main-sheet to leeward cleat, or takes a turn round cleat and holds sheet in his hand.
2. The crew: provides himself with two reef ties, and slacks off kicking strap.

## II.   Lower the mainsail

Partially or fully.

### a)  If partially lowered:
Helmsman watches his course.

Sail lowered as far as second reef if only one reef to be taken in.
Lowered to third reef if two are to be taken in.
Crew lashes down:
  1)  The tack of sail with a reef tie, or hooks it down.
  2)  The clew of sail.

**Details of outhaul:**
(one of many systems)

Haul cringle in leech of sail towards outboard end of boom, with several turns of the line through the cringle as in a block and tackle.

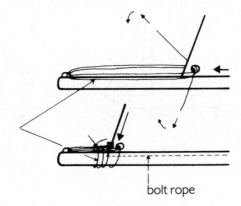

bolt rope

Tie it with reef knot (not too tight if there are several turns).
Take a few turns round boom with rest of line to keep bolt-rope in place.

### b)  Lower mainsail altogether:
  If crew tired.
  If crew makes heavy work with a billowing sail.
  This lets helmsman steer a convenient course under headsail only.

## III.   Hoist mainsail

Heading to windward.
Then, without hurry:
  Roll up foot of sail.
  Tie reef points (with a slip reef).

# ——Shaking out a Reef——

**Turn to windward**

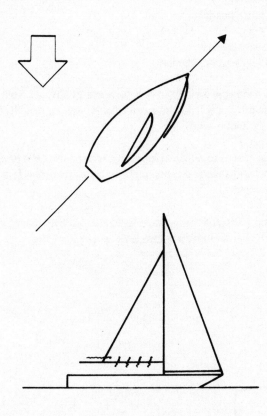

Helmsman makes fast main sheet and watches his course.

**Crew:**
    Unties all reef points.
    Casts off clew cringle.
    Slacks off kicking strap.
    Slacks off clew outhaul.

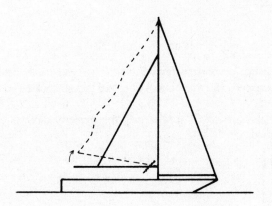

Casts off tack cringle.
Rehoists mainsail (taking up weight of boom with topping lift).
Hardens up mainsail outhaul and kicking strap.

# —— Picking up a Mooring ——

Wind abeam.
Crew for'ard with: Boathook.
Warp.

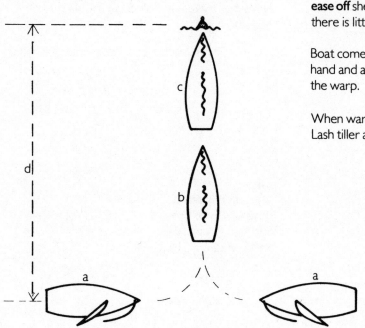

Put yourself in position (a)
**Downwind** of the mooring by a distance (d) which will depend on:

    Boat's headway.
    Wind.
    Sea state.
    Helmsman's judgment.

Turn into the wind (b). While turning into wind gradually **ease off** sheets. If necessary raise boom with topping lift (if there is little wind).

Boat comes to a stop at (c). Crew, with boathook in one hand and a warp in other, picks up buoy and makes fast the warp.

When warp has been made fast, lower jib, then mainsail. Lash tiller amidships before leaving vessel.

## Remarks

Do not lower sail when you are held by boathook only.
Do not pick up a buoy astern; if you go past it, recommence.

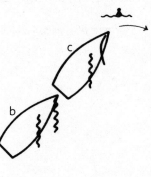

Do not lower jib before you have lost all way. It will enable you to repeat manoeuvre on either tack (by putting jib aback).
Make a habit of approaching the mooring **directly upwind.**

**Otherwise,**
with the sheets slack (b), the boat will stop short of the buoy (c). Jib has been backed but angle of boat to wind makes it ineffective and boat drifts onto obstacle.

# —— Man Overboard ——

If someone falls into the water:
    Throw him a **lifebuoy.**
    One of crew **keeps him in sight.**
    Another **notes compass course** and **exact time.**

Manoeuvre boat so that the wind is **abeam** or **a little for'ard**
Get a warp ready with a big loop (bowline knot) at end.

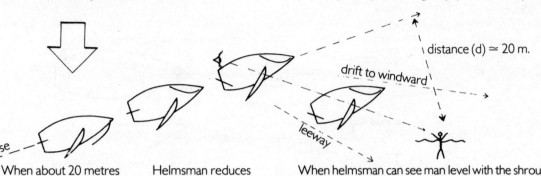

When about 20 metres upwind from man in water:

Helmsman reduces speed, jib put aback.

When helmsman can see man level with the shrouds, he takes all way off boat by putting down the helm, heaves-to (p. V) and lets her drift.

*Note*
If you are drifting to leeward of the man, put helm briefly amidships, then heave-to again.
If you drift to windward you must begin manoeuvre again.

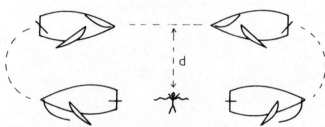

## ON A REACH

Turn into wind as soon as man falls overboard.
(You can rescue him in less than a minute.)

## ON A CLOSE REACH

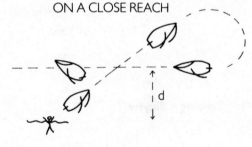

Or sail on and then gybe.

## ON A BROAD REACH

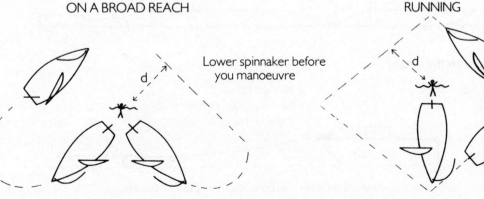

Lower spinnaker before you manoeuvre

## RUNNING

# — Towing —

## I.  Towing another boat

**Towing warp:**
At least 10 m. long, with spring if possible.
Warp belonging to towed boat preferably.
Secure with knot that is **easily cast off.**

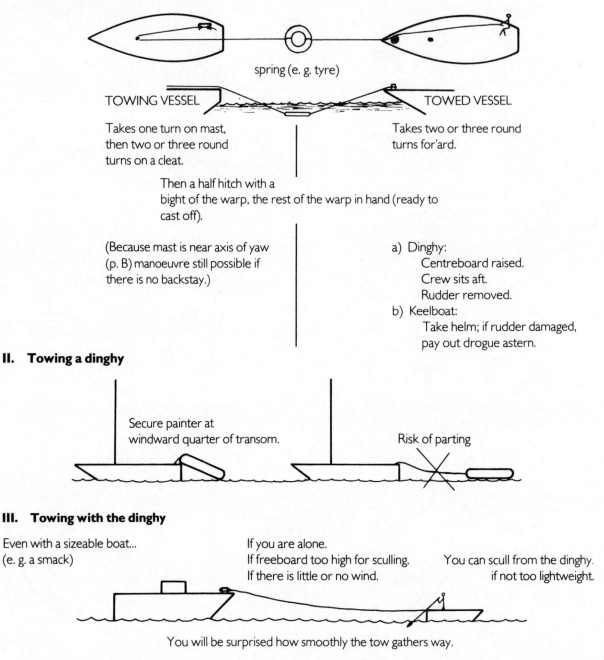

spring (e. g. tyre)

TOWING VESSEL                                                    TOWED VESSEL

Takes one turn on mast,                          Takes two or three round
then two or three round                          turns for'ard.
turns on a cleat.

Then a half hitch with a
bight of the warp, the rest of the warp in hand (ready to
cast off).

(Because mast is near axis of yaw          a)  Dinghy:
(p. B) manoeuvre still possible if                  Centreboard raised.
there is no backstay.)                                 Crew sits aft.
                                                                   Rudder removed.
                                                           b)  Keelboat:
                                                                   Take helm; if rudder damaged,
                                                                   pay out drogue astern.

## II.  Towing a dinghy

Secure painter at                                      Risk of parting
windward quarter of transom.

## III.  Towing with the dinghy

Even with a sizeable boat...          If you are alone.
(e. g. a smack)                            If freeboard too high for sculling.          You can scull from the dinghy.
                                                  If there is little or no wind.                  if not too lightweight.

You will be surprised how smoothly the tow gathers way.

## IV.  Towing with the dinghy

(inflatable)

**Pushing:**
Effective, even off-shore.

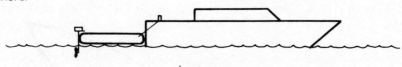

short warp

**Pulling:**
In a flat calm.

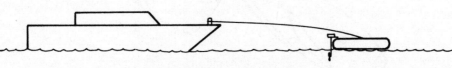

Secure at stemhead if possible.
If necessary tow by going astern.

**Dinghy alongside:**
Only in smooth water, and not advisable.

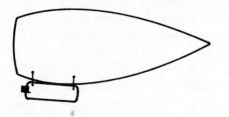

## V.  Two boats alongside

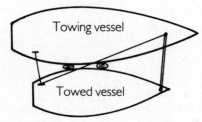

Towing vessel

Towed vessel

The towed vessel gets strong warps ready:
    One after breast-rope
    One after spring
    One for'ard breast-rope, which should be doubled,
        because if towing vessel accelerates suddenly at
        speed, the strain will be considerable.
If for'ard breast-rope should part the consequences
would be serious.

# Going Alongside Another Vessel

**Under way**

Go alongside on a CLOSE REACH

1 m.

**The approaching vessel:**
Helmsman steers **to windward** of other vessel.
Adjusts his **speed** by trimming mainsail (with the sheet in his hand) throughout the manoeuvre.
**Watches** stern of other boat.
Comes alongside not more than one metre for'ard of her stern.
Crew on foredeck ready to fend off.

**The vessel approached:**
Maintains constant but reduced **speed** (with jib slightly aback).
Maintains her **course**.
Helmsman must not look astern.
Crew near helmsman ready to fend off.

**When casting off from another vessel:**
It is vessel approached that moves first –
  by letting her jib fill,
  and turning off the wind.

*Note*
NEVER DO THIS

If you approach **to leeward**:
Others vessel's boom may foul your shrouds.

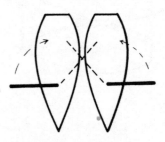

If you approach **downwind**:
Any rolling will lead to a gybe.

# ——Going Alongside Another Vessel——

**At a mooring**

(with owner's permission)

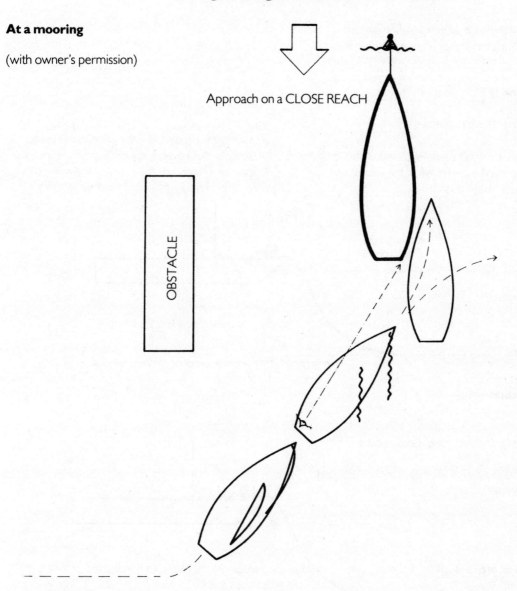

Approach on a CLOSE REACH

OBSTACLE

Come alongside:
   On side opposite to that from which you are
      approaching.
   Opposite to any obstacle.

Throughout the manoeuvre helmsman must have an
unobstructed view and must keep his eye on stern of
vessel approached.
   If manoeuvre cannot be completed, you must put up
your helm and turn off wind.

# Anchoring

Whenever you anchor in a difficult situation pay out a
tripping line and buoy the anchor (in case you have to slip).

## The tripping line

(To free a fouled anchor by upsetting it.)

The tripping line (of small diameter to reduce the drag
in a current) is bent on to the **crown** of the anchor and
made fast to a buoy, or on board.

Lay out the line on deck like the cable, but separate
from it, and pay it out over the pulpit as you veer the cable.
(The part of a nylon line that is out of the water should
be protected from sunlight with a black vinyl tube.)

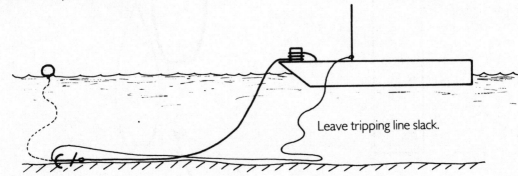

Leave tripping line slack.

## Backing an anchor

Very effective:
    If you are drifting on shore (dismasted, rudder broken,
      etc.).
    If you doubt the security of your main anchor (e.g. bad
      weather forecast).

## Anchor fore and aft

Kedge anchor + main anchor = anchor of twice the
weight of main anchor.

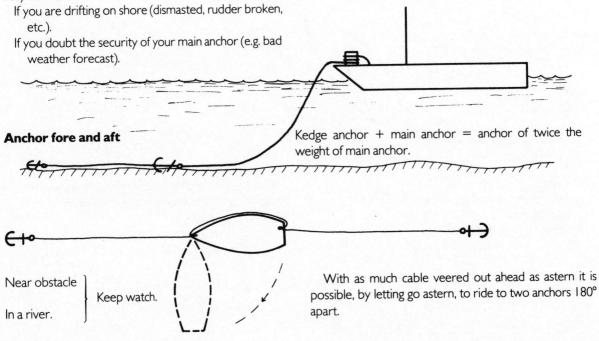

Near obstacle
In a river.     }   Keep watch.

With as much cable veered out ahead as astern it is
possible, by letting go astern, to ride to two anchors 180°
apart.

# — Anchoring —

## Riding to two anchors

This reduces the swinging circle due to wind or current.
  In moderate winds reduce angle between cables.
  In strong winds anchoring in this way is inadvisable.

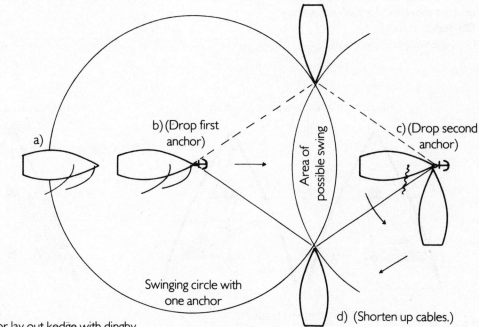

a)

b) (Drop first anchor)

Area of possible swing

c) (Drop second anchor)

Swinging circle with one anchor

d) (Shorten up cables.)

Flying moor (a, b, c, d) or lay out kedge with dinghy.

## Plumb-line anchoring

When main anchor is likely to drag.

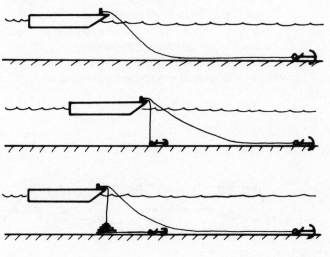

Precautionary measure in a squall (or if impossible to back the anchor).
  Dropping a second anchor.

1. First position, moored to main anchor.

2. Heave in some of the cable.
   Drop second anchor clear of the run of the first.

3. Return to first position.
   Lower second cable in a heap.

Anchoring in a harbour inadvisable, often illegal.
Make sure that the chain shackles are secure.

**Nature of bottom:**
If rocky, or doubtful, attach a **tripping line**.

**In relation to shore:**
If high wind experienced or expected, do not anchor
**on a lee shore;** or else **back the anchor.**

**On deck:**
One crew-member, in boots.

Anchor chain ready in a coil (slight heel).

or ranged on deck (steep heel).

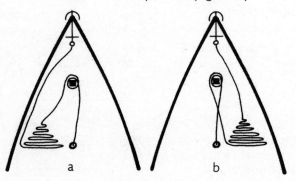

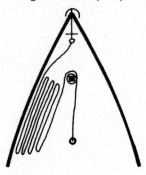

Two stages: Upset the coil, so that end made fast to
anchor is on top and will run easily.

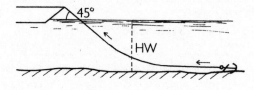

Never veer all the chain out of the locker; leave at least 2
or 3 metres.
> 'Theoretically' the amount of chain veered out should
> be at least three times depth at High Water.
> 'In practice', at night with the crew asleep, veer it all out
> except of course the last two metres.

With chain pulling at 45° to horizontal at the bows it
should, because of its weight, be horizontal at the anchor.

**The samson post:**
Three round turns on the samson post are enough.
The top turn leading to the chain pipe.

Chain pipe

Cable hold fast

# —— To Anchor ——

## Upwind

Turn into wind (as in picking up a mooring).
Mainsail up. (The sail furthest aft, makes it easier to drop astern.)
With or without jib.

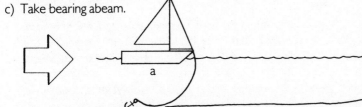

a) Boat turns into the wind, the sails shiver and then she stops.
At this moment crew lets go anchor on helmsman's command.

b) Boat makes sternway.
Crew veers out cable.

c) Operation complete. Make sure anchor is holding by taking a bearing abeam (two marks in transit).

## Downwind

a) Drop anchor under sail or under bare poles.
b) Veer out cable. Helmsman turns into wind before all cable is veered out.
c) Take bearing abeam.

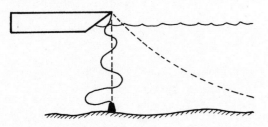

## In fog or at night

When not possible to take bearing.
Lower sounding lead from bow and allow some slack. Feel the line every 5 or 10 minutes without lifting the lead off the bottom:

> If line is vertical your anchor is holding.
> If line slopes away ahead you are **dragging**.

At night, when at anchor in an open roadstead, do not forget your riding lights; or display a hurricane lantern in the shrouds.

# ——At the Anchorage——

To avoid going aground.
The method of calculation is the same if you want to
discover the necessary depth before you anchor.
   Watch echo-sounder until it shows this depth, then
drop anchor.

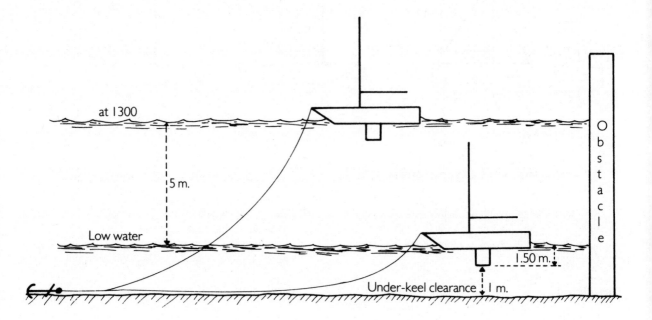

## 1. Calculate

(see p. W)

Time 1300.

| | |
|---|---|
| Calculated height of tide | 7.00 m. |
| (From Tide Table) Height at next | |
| Low Water... | − 1.95 |
| Therefore fall of | 5.05 (say 5 m.) |
| Your draught | + 1.50 |
| Allow under-keel clearance | + 1.00 |
| Total | 7.50 m. |

## 2. Sound

For safety the echo-sounder should therefore read **at
least 7.50 metres.** If it reads 6.50 you are going to touch
bottom. If it reads 4.00 it is time to **anchor elsewhere.**
*Note*
i) Swinging circle larger at Low Water, so look out for
   obstacles (or less water if there is a sloping bottom).
ii) If possible, enquire about isolated under-water
   obstructions not shown on chart or mentioned in
   sailing directions.

# —Beaching—

For a picnic, to disembark one of the crew (or less often the skipper) or for any other reason.

The operation should be done on a rising tide; look out for breakers and do not let vessel bump on bottom.

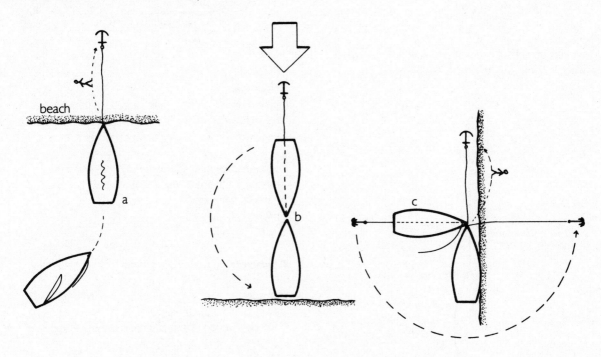

a) **Head-wind**

Leave mainsail up, and possibly jib.

Run her onto beach and lower sails.

One of crew then carries anchor ashore.

b) **Wind astern**

Come in under bare poles or with jib only.

Drop anchor before you go in and veer out part of cable. Let boat swing through 180° then disembark.

If one of crew remains on board he can veer out more cable when you come back.

If everybody goes ashore, remember the dinghy to get on board again!

c) **Wind abeam**

Come in under mainsail or genoa.

Drop kedge.

Run her onto beach and lower sails.

One of the crew goes ashore and carries sheet anchor to windward.

If there are breakers, heave in kedge. It will later be carried ashore to bring boat in when shore party returns.

**Set an anchor watch while you are ashore.**

# —— Going Aground ——

## On passage

(Due to boat being out of control on a lee shore.)

Prepare to **back the anchor.**

*Note*
You may be able to check shoreward drift with a sea anchor before you can drop sheet anchor.

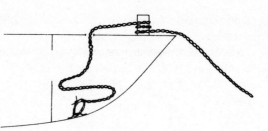

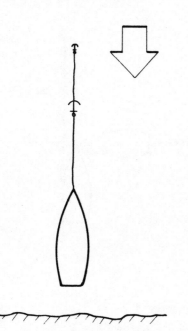

## At anchor

(Dragging anchor.)

If you cannot use the dinghy to lay out a **second anchor.**
If a **plumb-line** anchorage not possible.
If wind too strong to haul in cable.

**Remember:**
Inboard end of anchor chain is secured to the hull with several turns of seizing. You can slip your anchor by cutting these with a knife. Never undo a shackle.

Prepare to leave anchorage:
a) Attach a tripping line and buoy to anchor chain.
b) Hoist mainsail and jib.
c) Cast off.

## At anchor

(Aground.)

In a rough sea do not go overboard before boat is aground.
In an attempt to get afloat:
    Hoist mainsail and jib.
    Give boat a list.
    Heave in the cable if possible.
    Be ready to slip anchor if necessary. (Mind your fingers!)

## Driven ashore

Never use legs to support boat in soft mud.
Never use legs on rocks; use mats to protect hull and lay out a warp, to windward or into the current, to get her off. (If you have a light strong plate about a metre across and roughly the shape of the keel it will be very useful should hull rest on a pointed rock !)
If the bottom is flat and smooth use the legs and anchor.

## Broken rudder

Put out a drogue or use a sweep.

## A leak

**Take the way off boat:** heave-to if possible – this lowers pressure of water and makes work on board easier.

**Stop hole:** with mattresses, clothing, etc.
**Bail:** with pump and bucket.
Carry out **emergency repairs:** with planks, doors, etc.
**Lay a course** for the nearest shelter.
  Instability due to the water in the bilges is important (see p. F).
  Put on life-jackets.
  Get the dinghy ready and check that the painter is secure.

## Leakage of gas or petrol

These form an explosive mixture with air – bail out with a bucket and ventilate.
Do not use any electrical equipment.
Do not start the engine.
Do not smoke.

## Fire

Close all openings before quenching fire.
Turn down-wind.(This reduces the relative wind.)

## Lightning

**Avoid storm centre.**
Join **mast** and **shrouds** with thick copper wire and let several metres of it trail astern.
Disconnect batteries.
Do not touch rigging or life-lines.
Do not lie on deck.
Do not go overboard.
**Stay below** (Faraday cage).

# —— Rough Weather ——

Every boat behaves differently, so practise your manoeuvres before bad weather sets in.

## The barometer

Wind is moderate.
You have not listened to weather forecast.
But the glass has fallen 5 mb. in 4 hours.
   **Beware!** Prepare for a strong blow (Force 10 upwards).
Reduce sail.
Sort things out below (kedge, warps, etc. all to hand).
Clear the deck.
Crew prepared, physically (clothes, warm food) and in
   morale (up to the skipper).

## Choice of course

Avoid lee shore, which is seldom free from danger. The identification of landmarks and the approach may be difficult.
It is wise to stand out to sea in a boat of any size if making harbour is difficult.
With some or all sail off, it is difficult to pick up a man overboard – so wear a **harness**.

## When the wind gets up

Reduce speed (easing the boat reduces the stress on both ship and crew).

## Reefing

With a rising sea, set a high-footed jib (to be clear of seas breaking over the bow).

## Keeping on course

Reduce the speed still further.

Mainsail and
backed jib

Under head sail only

## Heaving-to

(Or lying a-hull under bare poles) is better than running before the wind in very severe weather.
Put the boat four points (45°) off the wind; with a beam wind she rolls, head-to-wind she pitches and slams.

   A well placed sea anchor helps to stabilize the boat
      (assuming a solidly built boat).
   Pouring oil to windward reduces breaking waves.

Safe angle to waves

Drift

## Running before the wind

Be sure you have enough sea room to leeward.
Take steps to avoid being swamped by breaking waves.
   This may happen because you are going too fast; when
   the boat is checked on the crest of a wave you risk
   broaching to and being rolled over.
Therefore, go slowly.

**Under jib only.**

**Under bare poles.** There will be enough wind resistance
   to keep the boat moving.
**Slower still** with sea anchor astern.
With a **stout warp as a drogue,** with or without some
   form of ballast. This keeps the boat from going off the
   wind and reduces speed. (The warp must be secure
   and the boat solidly built – keep a knife handy.)

With the drogue for'ard:
Boat makes sternway.
Rudder is under stress (and must be immobilized).

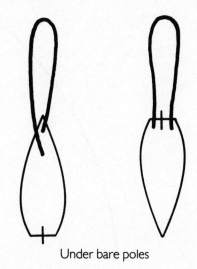

Under bare poles

With the drogue astern:
Keep cabin door shut (in case of a sea coming on board).

   If she is making too much way, steer 20° off the wind to
   avoid pitching into the wave ahead.
To heave in the warp, first cast off one end.

# —Spinnaker—
### (Not essential for coastal cruising.)

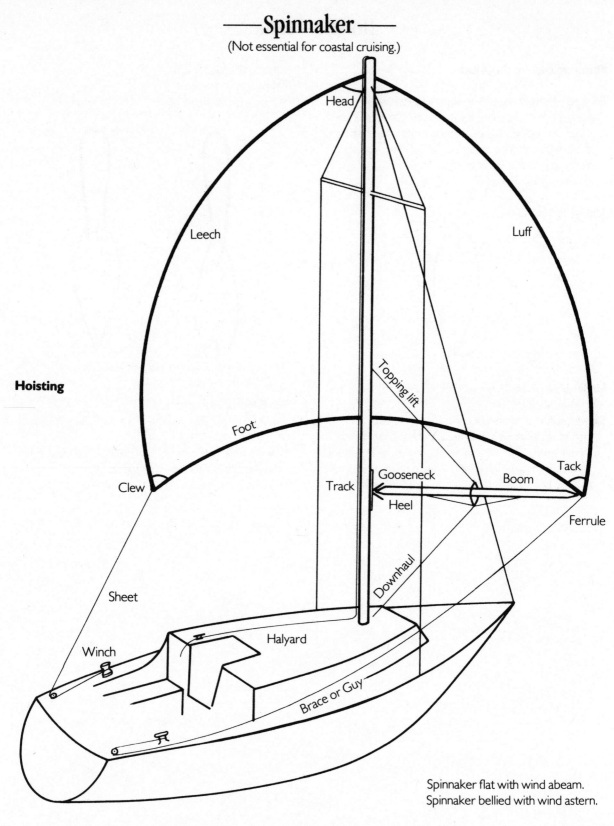

**Hoisting**

Head

Leech

Luff

Foot

Topping lift

Clew

Gooseneck

Track

Boom

Tack

Heel

Ferrule

Sheet

Downhaul

Winch

Halyard

Brace or Guy

Spinnaker flat with wind abeam.
Spinnaker bellied with wind astern.

# ——Spinnaker——

**Preparation**

**Folding the spinnaker**

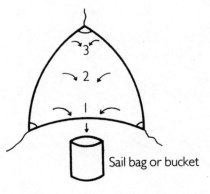

Sail bag or bucket

Setting the spinnaker in stops, if there is much wind

**Setting the spinnaker**

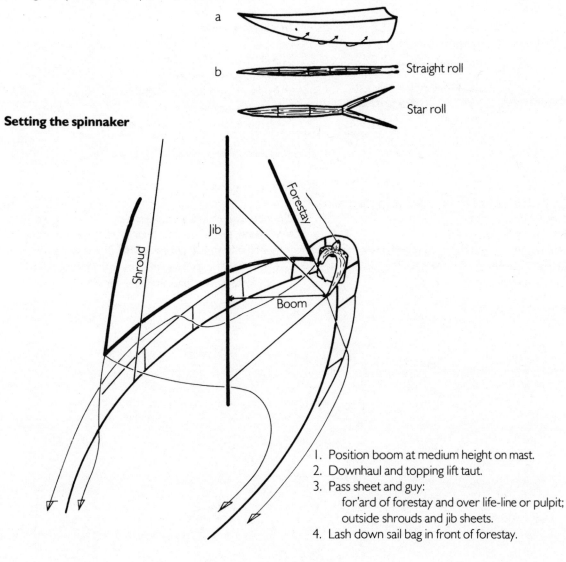

a

b — Straight roll

Star roll

Forestay

Jib

Shroud

Boom

1. Position boom at medium height on mast.
2. Downhaul and topping lift taut.
3. Pass sheet and guy:
   for'ard of forestay and over life-line or pulpit;
   outside shrouds and jib sheets.
4. Lash down sail bag in front of forestay.

# — Spinnaker —

**Point of sailing**

On a reach
(moderate wind)

(with mainsail and jib)

On a broad reach
(strong wind)

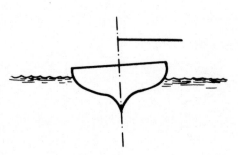

Spinnaker boom braced horizontal and perpendicular to
   relative wind.
Downhaul made fast on winch.
One crew member stands by the guy and sheet.
Another crew member hoists spinnaker rapidly and
   lowers jib, furling it when spinnaker fills.

**In a strong wind**

The spinnaker is kept flat:
   by hauling in the sheet;
   by slacking off the guy a little;
   by lowering the boom.
The jib, well sheeted-in, will keep her from luffing up.

**In a heavy sea**

If boat begins to luff: ease the sheet.
With wind abeam, or on a broad reach, the trim may
   become unstable; put her a little off the wind.
Do not belay the guy; a good crew can pay out the guy
   rapidly to lower spinnaker in emergency.

# —— Spinnaker ——

## Sailing by the lee

1. Wind astern.
2. Lower foresails (jib, genoa, etc.).
3. Slacken off spinnaker-boom downhaul.

4. Haul on sheet.
   Disengage boom from gooseneck spinnaker.

5. Bring spinnaker boom across to clew.
   Put mainsail over on other tack.

6. Engage boom ferrule to mast.
   Pay out new sheet (guy) gently.

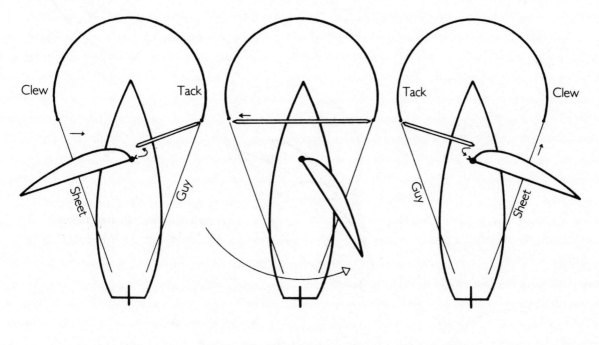

*Note*

The balance of the tiller will show you how the spinnaker is pulling (p.T)

A burgee is indispensable with a spinnaker.

# —— Spinnaker ——

**Lowering the spinnaker**

3. The spinnaker collapsed:
   One crew member at halyard lowers spinnaker gently.
   Anothers gathers it in beneath boom and stows it below.

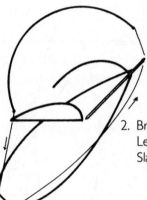

2. Bring spinnaker boom up to forestay.
   Let out main sheet as far as possible.
   Slacken off guy, or let fly tack of spinnaker.

1. Come on to a broad reach.
   Hoist jib or genoa (to windward of spinnaker).

# —— Return to Harbour ——

## Preparatory

Come in under mainsail and jib (not genoa).

## On foredeck:
Crew member with boathook;
A warp flaked down (with free end temporarily made fast to pulpit).
Another crew member ready to lower or rehoist sails.
One or two fenders on each side.
The deck clear.
Hoist the appropriate flags:
    Courtesy flag
    Club burgee
    National ensign, pratique, etc.

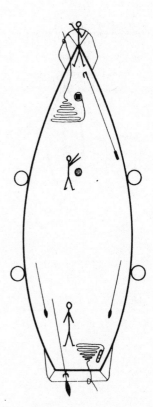

## Aft:
Crew member with a sweep ready (for forward propulsion,) two fair-sized paddles, or two oars (for moving the boat either ahead or astern – effective but seldom used).
A warp flaked down.

## At the landing place:
1. Come in under mainsail and jib (for good steerage way – there may be obstacles to avoid).
2. Make a reconnaisance by doing a 'tour of the harbour', noting:
    selected berth
    wind direction
    any obstructions.
    To reduce speed lower jib (not mainsail) to give helmsman clearer view, and man for'ard can look around without hindrance.
3. Mooring may be direct (to quay), or indirect (to a buoy or a moored boat).

## Note
If you are staying on board for a meal avoid mooring with the wind astern. The open cabin door, the wind, the cold and humidity will make things unpleasant.

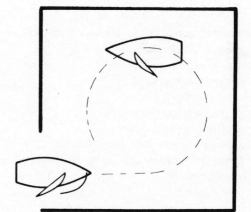

# —— Return to Harbour ——

**Upwind**

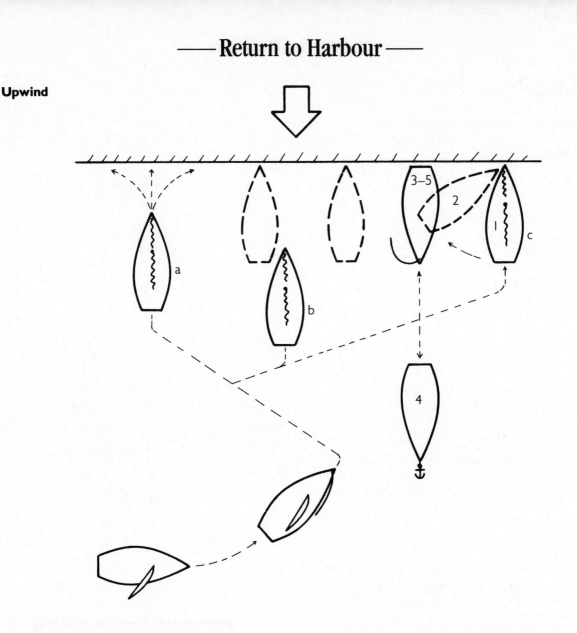

**Tack towards quay:** if there is little wind hoist jib as well, to increase speed and reduce leeway.

**Final stage:** be prepared to lower sail(s) immediately.

a) As in picking up a buoy:
    Turn to port or starboard
        if you have too much way on boat,
        if there is enough room.

b) Coming in between two moored boats:
    Helmsman should try to bring her to a stand-still level with their sterns.

The man for'ard is ready and makes fast – but only if she is not carrying too much way!

c) If it is necessary to put an anchor out:
    1) Come up to quay, make fast and lower sails.
    2) Turn boat round.
    3) Make fast astern and pay out warp till you are in position to drop anchor (with tripping line), hoisting jib if necessary, at (4).
    4) Anchor and haul on stern warp to bring her back to quay (5).

**Variable headwind and obstruction**

### First Attempt

With mainsail and jib, bring her into wind (classic manoeuvre).
If boat comes to a stop before you reach quay, haul jib aback and try again.

ROCKS

But suppose wind changes.

### Second Attempt

The classic error is to fall back along same course with sails flapping (off the boat's centre-line). If she comes to a stop before you reach quay it is then impossible to put jib aback, boat falls from wind and strikes rocks.

### Therefore

always keep the boat **head to wind** with the jib up if in the vicinity of an obstruction.

## Downwind

Make 360° turn and lower mainsail.
Steer for mooring under bare poles, or with jib if there is little wind. Prepare to drop anchor (with tripping line).

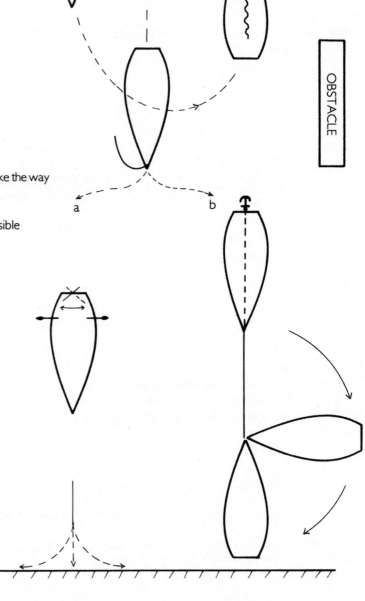

a) When not less than 50 metres from quay, take the way off boat:
   By lowering sail.
   By putting helm over slowly as far as possible (see p. J).
   By having crew row 'full astern'.

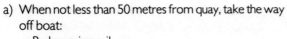

b) If anchoring is compulsory:
   Anchor with the wind astern.
   Stop boat and turn her round.

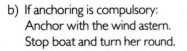

# —— Return to Harbour ——

**Wind abeam**

Come in under mainsail, ready to lower it immediately.

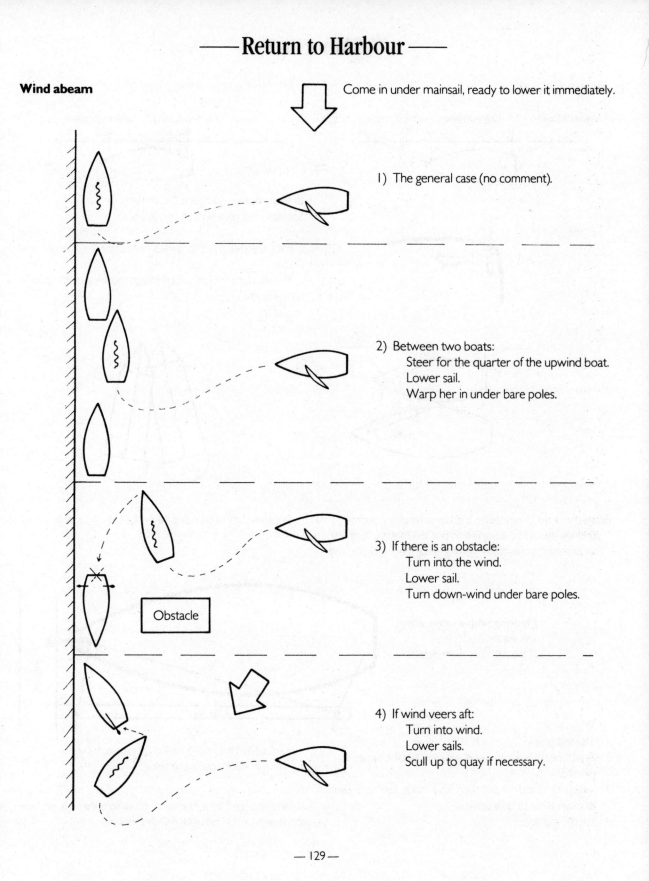

1) The general case (no comment).

2) Between two boats:
   Steer for the quarter of the upwind boat.
   Lower sail.
   Warp her in under bare poles.

3) If there is an obstacle:
   Turn into the wind.
   Lower sail.
   Turn down-wind under bare poles.

Obstacle

4) If wind veers aft:
   Turn into wind.
   Lower sails.
   Scull up to quay if necessary.

## Alongside pontoon

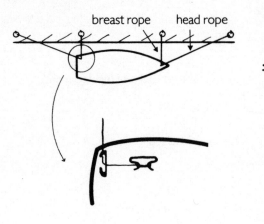

breast rope    head rope

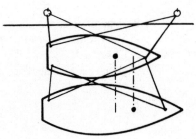

=

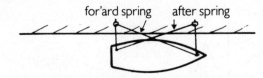

for'ard spring    after spring

**Breast ropes** limit lateral movement.
**Springs** limit fore and aft movement.
*Note*
Cleats are designed to take strain along their length, not across.

Breast rope should pass through mooring chock parallel to transom.

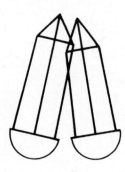

Boats moored alongside (at a quay or mooring buoy):
Springs should be adjusted to put the masts out of line, to prevent cross-trees getting entangled if boats roll.

(Warps should be hove taut especially in strong wind.)

**Mooring with a single warp:**
this leaves deck clear.
(One of many methods.)

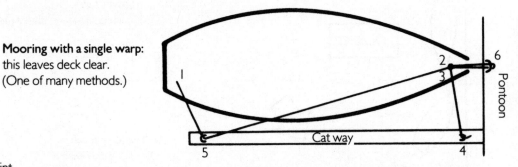

Pontoon

Cat way

1. Starting point.
2. A half-hitch, but leave enough slack to take up at point 5.
3. Warp doubled to pontoon and made fast at 2, with enough slack to take up at 6.
4. Finishing point.

5. Get boat into final position and make fast at 5.
6. Take in slack and make fast at 6.

*Note*
When moored to a pontoon, or where there is no tide, the warp can be hove taut with the winch.

# Mooring

## Alongside quay

Moor near a ladder if possible.
Double head and stern ropes (long, to act as shock absorbers).

Boat can move ahead and astern. To limit this movement, ideal solution is to make warps fast, at Half Tide, to the ladders.

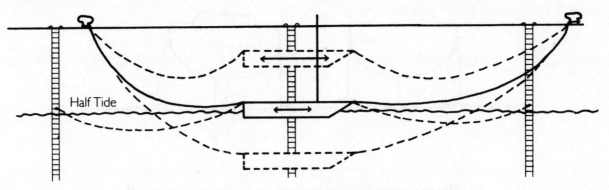

Half Tide

Enquire whether there are any sewage outfalls.
Make one breast rope fast to quay or to a ladder.
Keep a watch on the boat, particularly at High Water, at Half Tide and when she takes the ground.
**When she takes the ground** boat should be upright or
have slight list towards the quay.
See that cross-trees do not foul quay.
Remember that fenders are slightly compressible and yield towards the wall.
Heave in warps gradually.

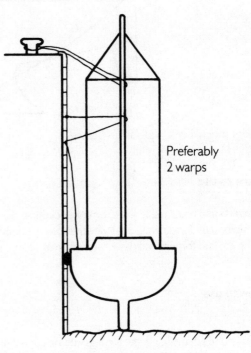

Preferably
2 warps

*Note*
If tidal range is decreasing and wind is steady, heave the warps taut at Low Water.

Do not moor alongside another boat if you are going to take the ground at Low Water.

If you take ground alongside a quay, keep a watch and expect to have to get up during the night.

Taking the ground alongside a quay is to be recommended for boats with deep keels as it is difficult to use legs.

# The Use of Legs

## The legs

When boat is upright, the shoes are above level of base of keel, in order to compensate for irregularities of the bottom.

normal position

leg

shoe

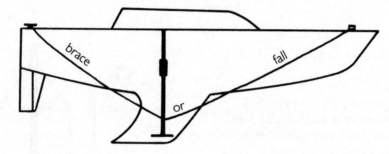

brace

or

fall

The legs should be vertical (adjust braces).

## Where to use

Bottom should be firm and free from obstructions.
If possible, seek local advice as to whether there is good holding ground for legs with your type of boat.

## When to use

### Case 1:
When you reach mooring; get the legs into position with their braces and supplementary warps.
**While boat is afloat:** Observe strain on warps; if there is much lateral movement, two warps or two anchors may be advisable.
**When berth dries out:** Check that the moorings are secure. Veer out plenty of chain and if possible cover crown of anchor with stones, particularly if there are other boats near the anchor.
Check that the legs are suitably placed.
    Examine the ground (for isolated rocks, etc. ).

### Case 2:
When cruising you may wish to careen the boat.
Get the legs and braces into position and take the ground with the ebb tide.

# ── The Use of Legs ──

When on legs the skipper will supervise the first grounding.
If bottom **slopes steeply:**
  Bow should point up the slope.

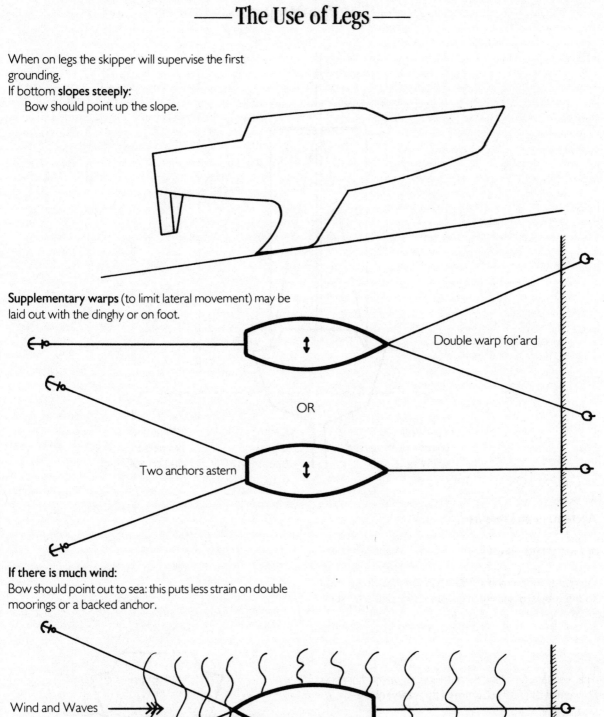

**Supplementary warps** (to limit lateral movement) may be laid out with the dinghy or on foot.

Double warp for'ard

OR

Two anchors astern

**If there is much wind:**
Bow should point out to sea: this puts less strain on double moorings or a backed anchor.

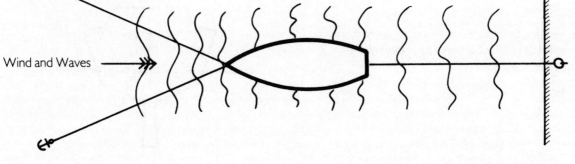

Wind and Waves →

# — The Boat —

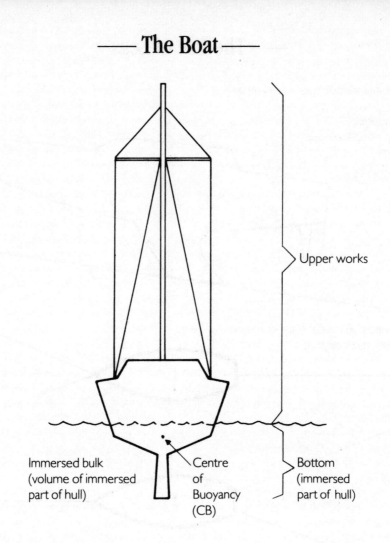

Upper works

Immersed bulk
(volume of immersed
part of hull)

Centre
of
Buoyancy
(CB)

Bottom
(immersed
part of hull)

## Archimedean Pressure

or Hydrostatic Thrust (HT)

Any body submerged in a liquid is subject to a force equal
to the weight of the liquid displaced (the displacement).

The resultant thrust is directed vertically upwards through
the centre of gravity (Centre of Buoyancy) of the
underwater volume of the hull.

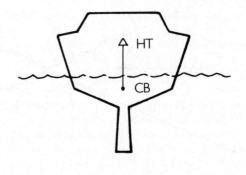

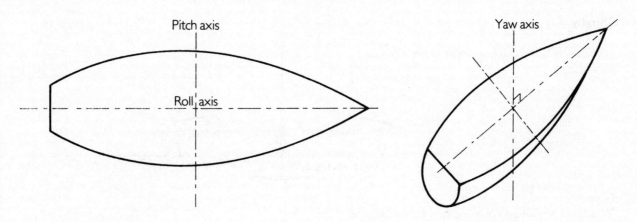

Displacement about the axes:

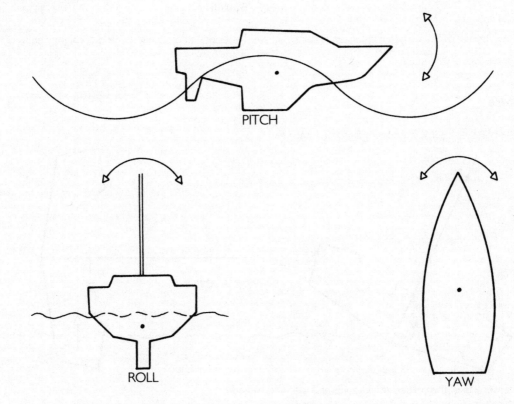

# ── Stability ──

## Dinghy

(In example, with no crew, centre of gravity CG is amidships.)

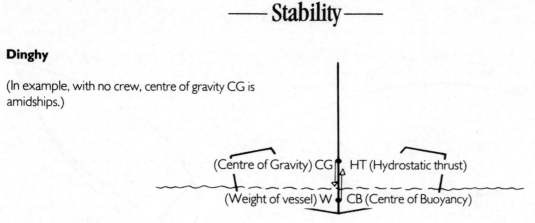

(Centre of Gravity) CG    HT (Hydrostatic thrust)

(Weight of vessel) W   CB (Centre of Buoyancy)

*Note*
W and HT are always equal and in opposite directions.
If the load increases the boat sinks deeper, increasing W and HT.

## Trim

Equilibrium position of boat when motionless in calm water.

## Stability

Tendency to return to original trim after being disturbed in any way.

## Metacentre

Transverse Metacentre (M): the limiting factor for stability.

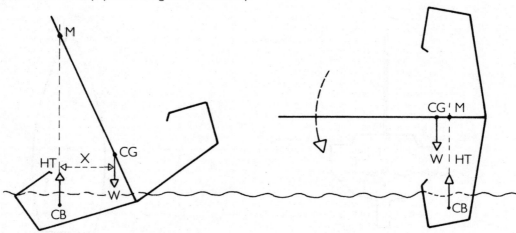

M is intersection of the vertical through CB and the plane of symmetry of the boat (here indicated by the mast; metacentre moves in this plane as boat heels.
    If CG is **below** M, stability is POSITIVE (the normal condition).
    If CG is **above** M, stability is NEGATIVE (capsize).

*Note*
The lower the centre of gravity (CG), the stronger the restoring couple X and the greater the stability.
When a boat heels the immersed volume and the centre of buoyancy are displaced.

**Keel boat**

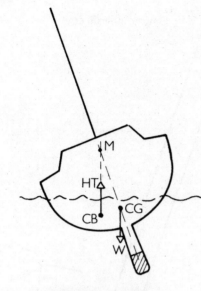

The deeper the keel,
the lower the centre of
gravity CG,
and the greater the stability.

Heeled over through 90°,
a keel boat still has POSITIVE
STABILITY. (Even with cabin door
open, water not shipped).

**Important note**

After being 'knocked down' (extremely rare), in a squall
for example, the keel comes out of the water. Its weight in
air is much greater than its weight in water.
The recovery of trim can be very quick and boat will
resume her course; so if you are pitched overboard, hang
on at once!

Boat will lose positive stability when heeled through about
120°
After that she will be rolled over.

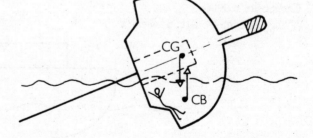

*Note*
Centre of gravity (CG) will have shifted with crew and
gear deposited on deckhead.

# —Stability—

## Stability of weight

(Keel boat)

## Stability of form

Dinghy, life-raft, etc.)

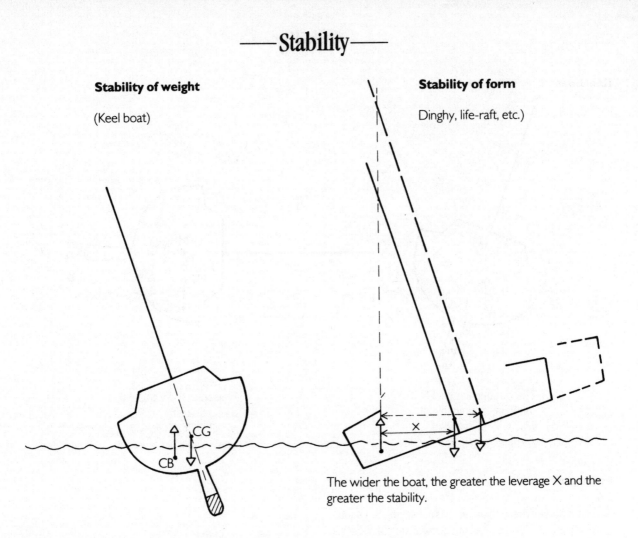

The wider the boat, the greater the leverage X and the greater the stability.

*Note*
With the crew sitting out, the centre of gravity CG is no longer in the median plane of the boat but displaced in their direction; the leverage X is therefore greater.

## Composite stability
(Weighted centre-board, trawlers, etc.)

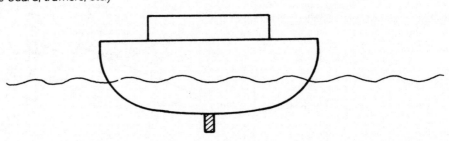

**Dead water in a boat is a danger**

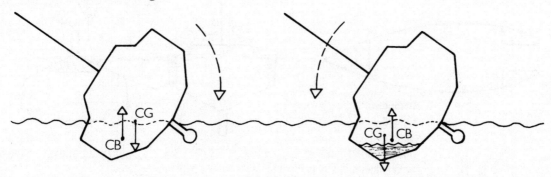

In a heavy roll:
Centre of Gravity CG is displaced to left because crew, taken unawares, have lurched in that direction. If X small, boat recovers slowly. Under the same conditions, and with one cubic metre of water in bilge (which weighs one ton) CG is displaced outside CB and result is a CAPSIZE.

**Remember**

The water in the bilge (dead water) can be compared to a ball of lead rolling with the list of the boat.

**Remedy**

For dinghies:    Self-bailers.
For keel boats: Avoid large openings.
                        Water-tight compartments.

          Transverse bulkheads                Longitudinal bulkheads

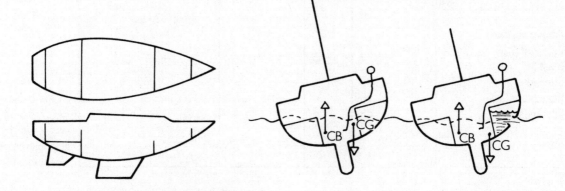

Water-tight bulkheads keep dead water in one place and stop it moving with boat, therefore little or no change in centre of gravity CG.

# —— Buoyancy Tanks ——

**Disposition:**

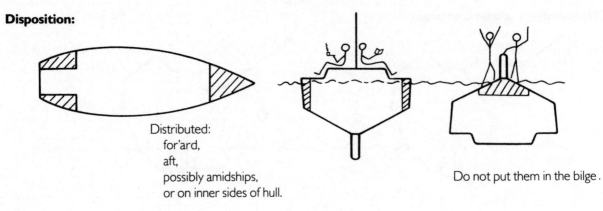

Distributed:
for'ard,
aft,
possibly amidships,
or on inner sides of hull.

Do not put them in the bilge.

## Calculation of the buoyancy reserve

example:
Weight/density ratio = Volume, (V) which is
approximately equal to Hydrostatic Thrust for
submerged objects.

## Materials

Polyvinyl, polystyrene, polyurethane or polyethylene
foam.

| Items and materials | | Weight (kg.) | Specific Gravity | Volume (Cu. decimetres*) | Reserve buoyancy required (m³) (W − V) |
|---|---|---|---|---|---|
| **Submerged** | | | | | |
| Hull | iron | 2000 | 7.88 | 253.8 | |
| Keel | lead | 400 | 11.34 | 35.3 | |
| Engine | alumin. | 50 | 2.70 | 18.5 | |
| Anchor | iron | 10 | 7.88 | 1.3 | |
| Chain, etc. | iron | 30 | 7.88 | 3.8 | |
| Total | | 2,490 | | 312.7 | 2.177 (= 2177 kg.) |
| **Above surface** | | | | | |
| Crew of 6 | | 480 | | | |
| Mast | | 50 | | | |
| Shrouds | | 10 | | | |
| Stanchions | | 30 | | | |
| Life-lines, etc. | | 15 | | | |
| Total | | 585 | | | 0.585 |
| | | | | Total | 2.762 m³ |

\* One cubic decimetre of water weighs approximately one kilogram.

*Notes:*
Natural timber floats of itself and does not enter
calculation.
Add buoyancy of air mattresses if these are available; e.g.,

$6 \times (2 \times 0.80 \times 0.10) = 0.960 \text{ m}^3 = 960 \text{ kg}.$
Above a certain tonnage it is difficult to provide the
necessary reserve buoyancy.
When a boat fills there may be buoyant air pockets.

—G—

# ——Fluids——
## (Fundamental principles)

## Theory

The resultant R of the pressure of a moving fluid (air or water) on a plane surface is perpendicular to the surface (a metal plate for example) whatever the direction of flow.

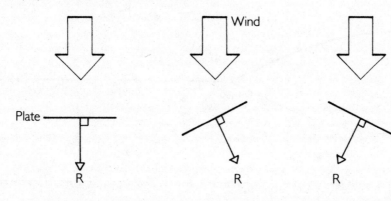

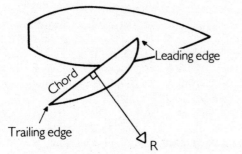

With a sail, the plane is the plane of the chord (the straight line joining the *leading edge* and the *trailing edge*).

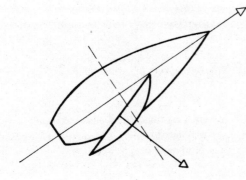

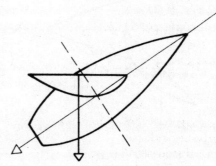

If R is directed backwards, in relation to the transverse axis of the boat, she will go astern.

# ——Components and Resultants——

Example of Parallelogram of Forces.

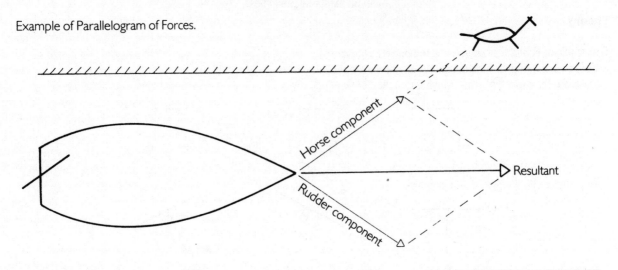

Therefore two components give resultant R

or

One resultant is compounded of two (or more)
components.

*Note*
In a sailing boat we are concerned only with the two
components parallel to the pitch and roll axes.

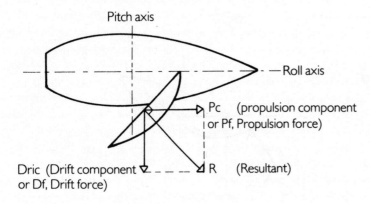

# — The Rudder Blade —

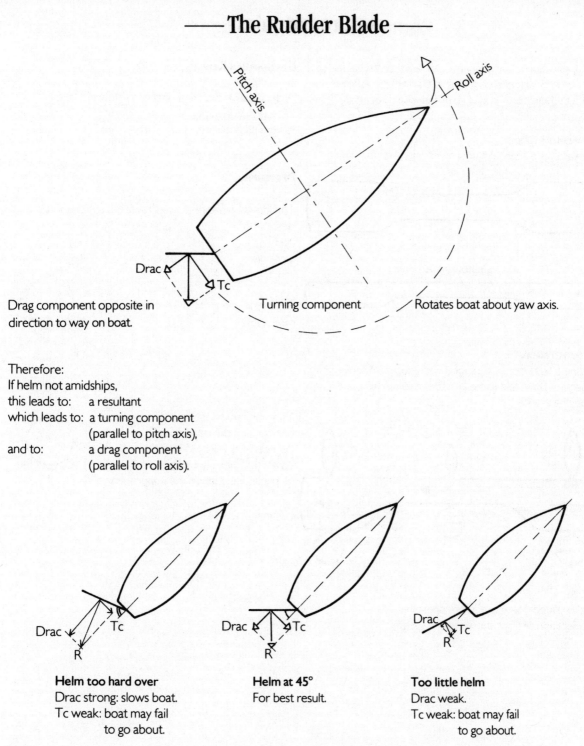

Pitch axis

Roll axis

Drac

Tc

Drag component opposite in direction to way on boat.

Turning component

Rotates boat about yaw axis.

Therefore:
If helm not amidships,
this leads to:     a resultant
which leads to:  a turning component
                 (parallel to pitch axis),
and to:          a drag component
                 (parallel to roll axis).

Drac   Tc   R

Drac   Tc   R

Drac   Tc   R

**Helm too hard over**
Drac strong: slows boat.
Tc weak: boat may fail
         to go about.

**Helm at 45°**
For best result.

**Too little helm**
Drac weak.
Tc weak: boat may fail
         to go about.

*Note*
There is always a Drag component, so every movement of helm has braking effect.

# — Aerodynamics —

The application of aerodynamics to sailing boats has led to the use on board of such terms as 'stalling', etc. A brief glance at their origin in aviation is therefore necessary.

## The Venturi tube:
for example, a channel with a constricted section.

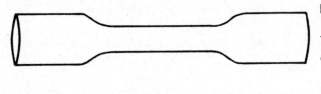

a half-venturi

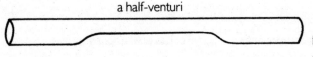

## Demonstration:
Imagine a half-venturi equipped with gauges (to show velocity of flow) and flame jets. Pass a stream of gas through the tube.

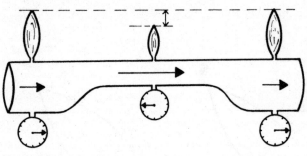

Notice:
Smaller flame, therefore lower pressure.
Acceleration of flow, shown by the gauges.

## Bernouilli's Law

A decrease in the cross-section of flow in a fluid increases its velocity, lowers its pressure.

## Pressure

The atmospheric pressure on a football is uniformly distributed.

Resting on the ground it is therefore motionless.

If for any reason the pressure on the upper part decreases, it will be displaced upwards. There is a 'depression' or partial vacuum on the upper surface.

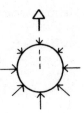

# —Aerodynamics—

## The Mistral

Air stream channeled between the mountains increases in velocity (Venturi effect) and gives rise to the local wind known as the Mistral in the South of France.

## The teaspoon

A teaspoon suspended between finger and thumb below a tap restricts cross-section of flow of water and produces a reduced pressure:
spoon clings to the water jet.

## The aircraft

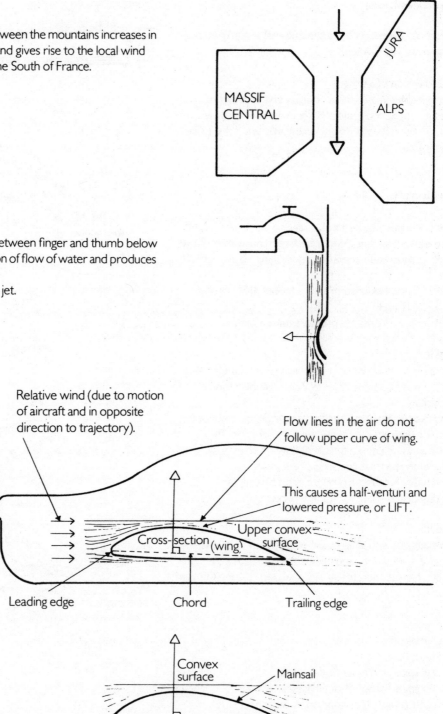

Relative wind (due to motion of aircraft and in opposite direction to trajectory).

Trajectory

Flow lines in the air do not follow upper curve of wing.

This causes a half-venturi and lowered pressure, or LIFT.

Upper convex surface

Cross-section (wing)

Leading edge

Chord

Trailing edge

## The sailing boat

Convex surface

Mainsail

Mast

Chord (in practice, the boom)

# —— The Aircraft ——

**Both air and water are fluids.**

### Some definitions

If you look down from a bridge at flow of stream past one of the piers you will see:

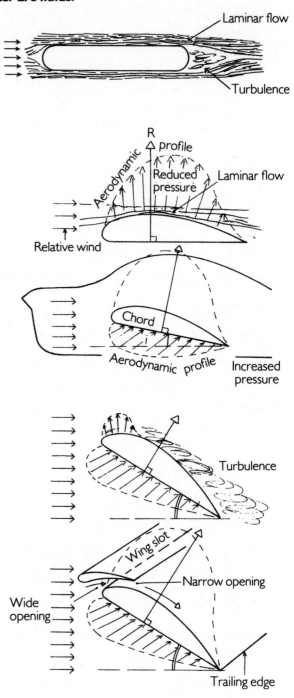

Laminar flow

Turbulence

### Cross-section of a wing:

Aerodynamic profile shows distribution of pressure measured at various points. R is the resultant aerodynamic force on aircraft wing. The reduced pressure is due to the laminar flow.

R

profile

Reduced pressure

Laminar flow

Aerodynamic

Relative wind

### The aircraft

**Case I:** Wing is attached to fuselage so that in level flight there is an angle of incidence $i$, between chord and relative wind. This increases pressure below wing, so increases R.

$$R = + \begin{array}{l} \text{Reduced pressure (about 4/5)} \\ \\ \text{Increased pressure (about 1/5)} \end{array}$$

Chord

$i$

Aerodynamic profile

Increased pressure

### Case II:

Aircraft is nose-up while continuing in level flight (so that relative wind is same); angle of incidence therefore increases.

Beyond a certain limit, this tilt makes angle of incidence too great for flow lines to follow the curve of wing. They 'break away', causing a turbulent flow which almost completely destroys reduced-pressure lift.

The smaller R causes aircraft to drop or 'stall' (a compulsory exercise for trainee-pilots).

Turbulence

### Case III:

Some aircraft with a high angle of incidence delay the stall by using a 'wing slot'. The principle is to create a Venturi effect which accelerates stream lines and restores laminar flow.

*Note*

R depends on

(i) rate of flow:

As speed increases, R increases.

As speed drops, R decreases.

(ii) 'depth' of wing (designed cross-section):

With increased depth, R increases.

With decreased depth, R decreases.

Wing slot

Narrow opening

Wide opening

Trailing edge

# —— The Sailing Boat ——

## Turbulent flow

(pressure sailing)

### Wind abeam

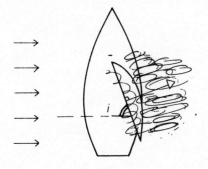

With helmsman who has 'forgotten' to ease the sheet
(angle *i* too big):
   excessive heel
   small Resultant, R,
(therefore less speed).

## Laminar flow

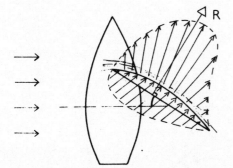

### Wind abeam

Sail correctly trimmed (to point where it just stops
flapping).
Small angle of incidence (necessary because it is pressure
that gives sail its curve).
Laminar flow on both inner and outer surface.
This gives the best result.

*Note*
A flapping sail impedes or destroys laminar flow.

### Wind astern

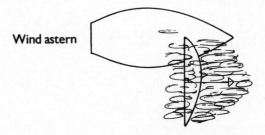

You will be able to observe laminar flow and turbulent
flow if you happen to sail when it is snowing.

## The jib

(Slotted wing principle)

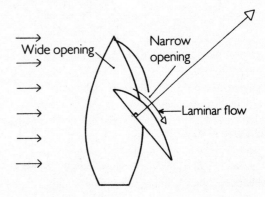

The Venturi effect increases the velocity of laminar flow,
therefore increases R.
**Note the formula:**
$R = C_2 (1/2\rho) \boxed{SV^2}$
Fear not: only two factors have to be remembered.
S = Surface area:
With twice the area of sail (and the wind unchanged) R is
twice as great.
$V^2$ = Velocity²
If wind speed doubles, R is not twice as big but four times
as big. This explains why dinghies capsize in squalls.

*Note*
A keel boat usually has two mainsails, one of them flat and
one full-bellied.
In light winds the bellied sail increases R.
In a strong wind the flat sail decreases R.

# —— Speed Wind  True Wind  Relative Wind ——

## On a windless day

A cyclist feels a wind on his face due to his movement:
opposite to his own direction,
its strength depending on his speed.

This wind is called SPEED WIND (SW)

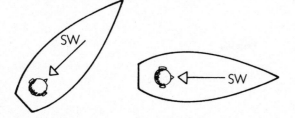

In a motor boat an observer would feel a speed wind SW,
in the same way.
Thus every moving vehicle creates a speed wind.

## On a windy day

If the TRUE WIND (TW), is regular in both force and
direction:

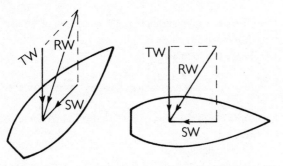

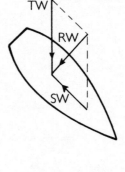

An observer on board would experience the resultant of
SW and TW.

This is the 'apparent wind' or RELATIVE WIND (RW),
also indicated by the burgee.

# — Speed Wind  True Wind  Relative Wind —

**The facts:**

For a boat moving at the same speed but on different points of sailing, the Relative Wind RW varies both in STRENGTH and DIRECTION.

A sailing boat will not move unless there is a True Wind (otherwise she is becalmed) but she makes use of the Relative Wind.

The nearer she points into the True Wind the stronger the Relative Wind; this explains why sand yachts can attain a speed of 75 mph in a 30 mph wind.

It is different for a sailing boat; the water resistance to the hull is 770 times as great as the air resistance.

Water is uncompressible and lacks the elasticity of air. The boat therefore needs a strong propulsive force Pf.

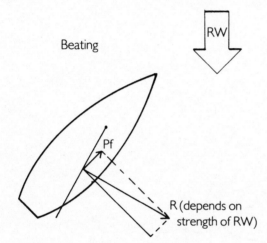

Beating

RW

Reaching

Pf

R (depends on strength of RW)

Pf

Resultant

With R smaller and Pf stronger, speed increases.

Close-hauled: Pf is small, speed low

Wind astern: speed of boat relatively low (reduced RW).

**N.B.**

1 Under sail only
SW1 ⟶ RW1

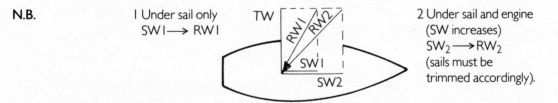

TW

RW1  RW2

SW1

SW2

2 Under sail and engine (SW increases)
SW2 ⟶ RW2
(sails must be trimmed accordingly).

The Relative Wind changes when boat rolls and at troughs and crests of waves.

# Centres of Application

**Centre of Effort** CE

Point of application of the resultant, R, of all wind forces acting on boat.

**Centre of Lateral Resistance** CLR

Point of application of the resultant of all water pressures acting on hull.

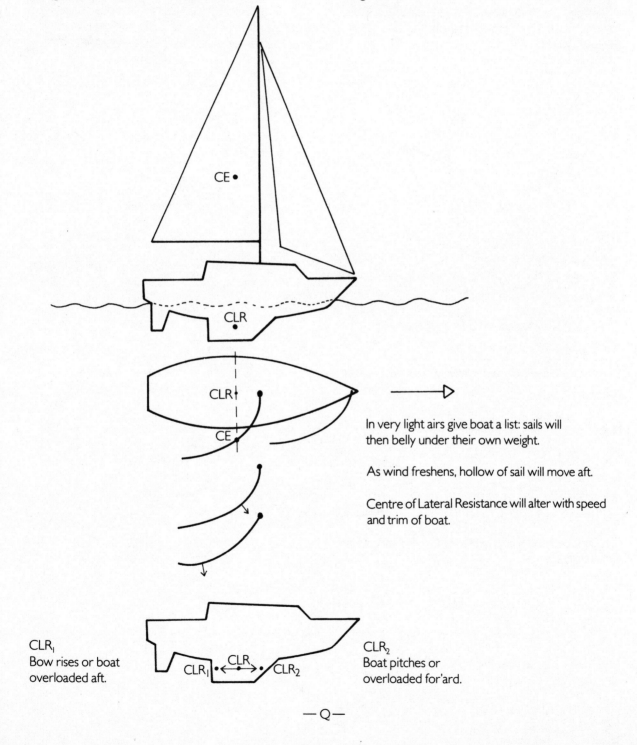

In very light airs give boat a list: sails will then belly under their own weight.

As wind freshens, hollow of sail will move aft.

Centre of Lateral Resistance will alter with speed and trim of boat.

CLR₁
Bow rises or boat overloaded aft.

CLR₂
Boat pitches or overloaded for'ard.

# —— Weather Helm and Lee Helm ——

**Close reach**

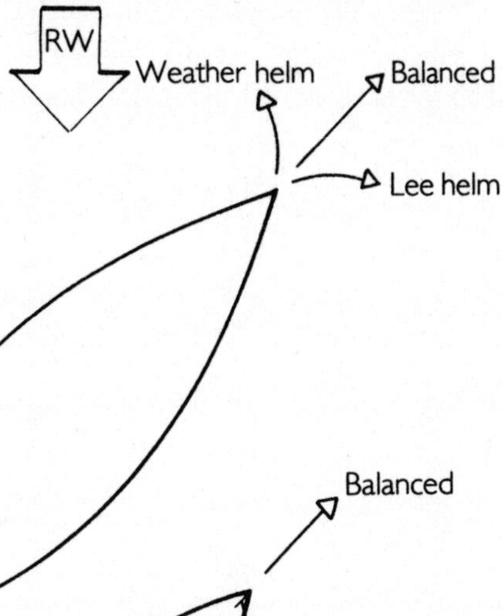

RW

Weather helm

Balanced

Lee helm

Balanced

**Cause**

CLR and CE in same plane

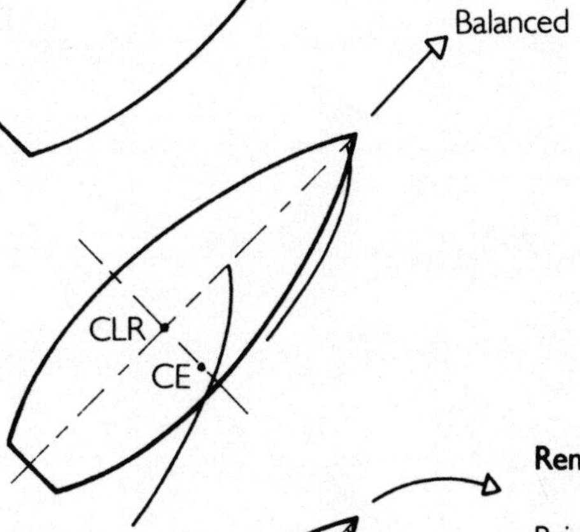

CLR
CE

**Remedy**

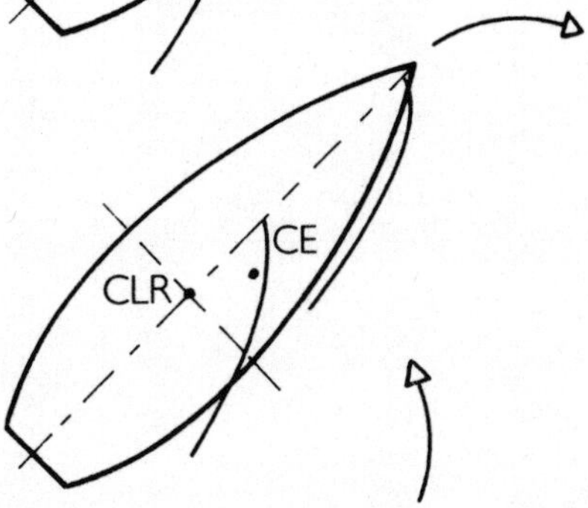

Bring CE aft by:
Lowering jib, or
Hoisting smaller jib, or
Increasing area of mainsail.

Too much sail for'ard

CLR
CE

Too much sail aft

CLR
CE

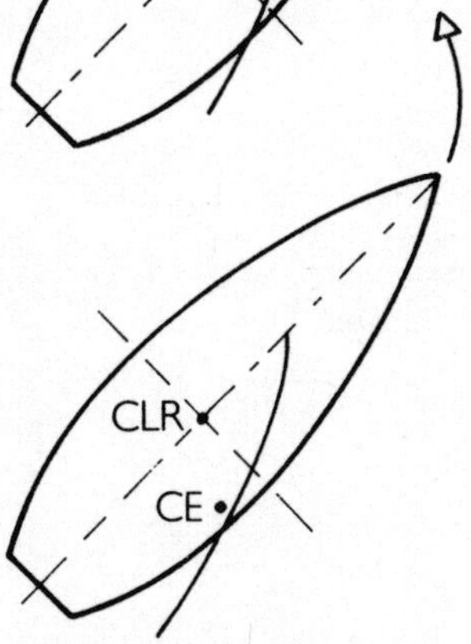

Bring CE forward by:
Hoisting jib, or
Substituting bigger jib, or
Reducing area of mainsail.

*Note*
A boat carrying weather helm can become balanced, or
carry lee helm, if load astern is increased.

**Wind astern**

With sails of unequal area, CE is off fore and aft axis of boat.

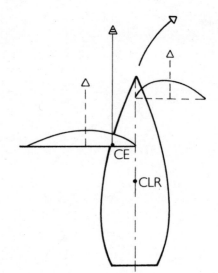

Helm has to be put more or less off centre to maintain trim with a following wind.

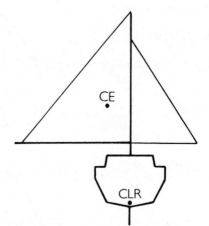

**Remedy**

Bring CE vertically above CLR, by:
Increasing area of foresail;
Reducing area of mainsail; or
Giving her a list (dinghy or small keel boat).

*Note*
A boat with a list draws less water.

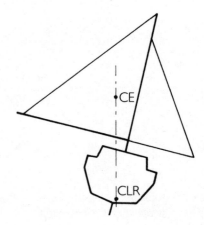

**Broad reach**

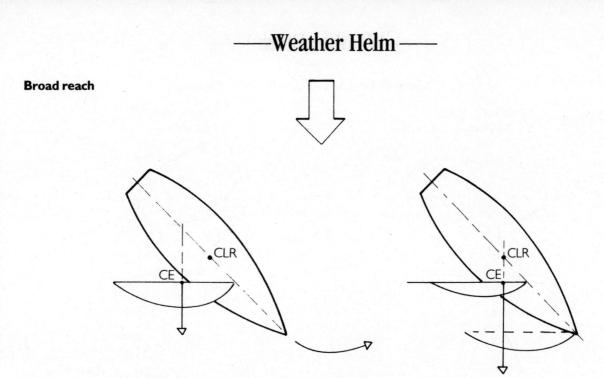

The line of action of the force acting on sail passes astern of the centre of lateral resistance CLR, giving boat weather helm.

**Remedy:**
Increase area of foresail, or
Take in a reef, even if you have genoa up.

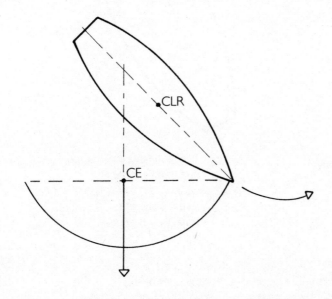

Spinnaker too widely open.

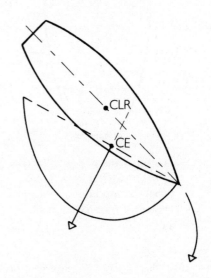

If sheeted in too hard it will give *lee helm*.

# Weather Helm

Every boat tends to carry weather helm when it has a list.

Underwater bulk
symmetrical:

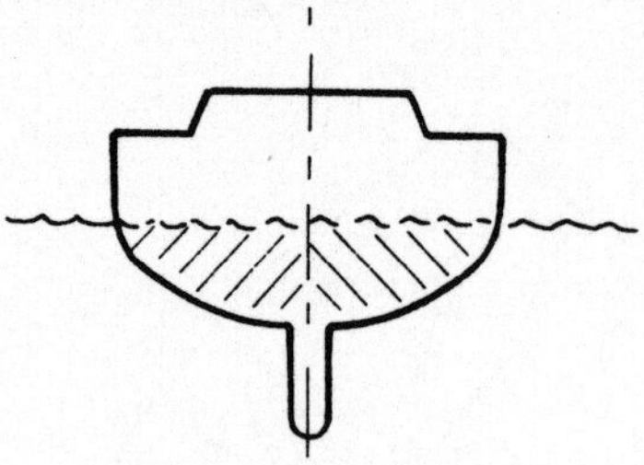

Underwater bulk
asymmetrical:

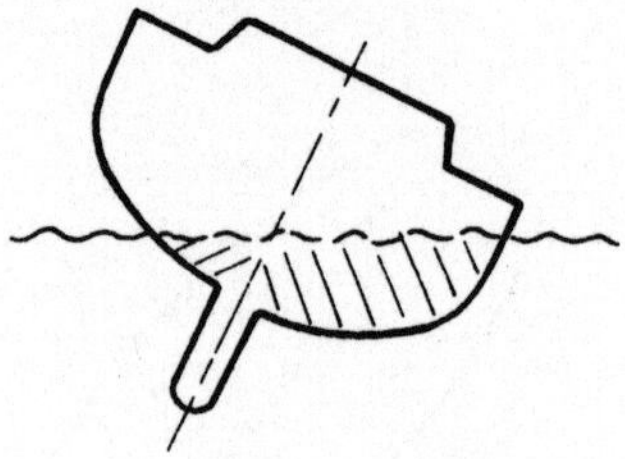

Boat on even keel.

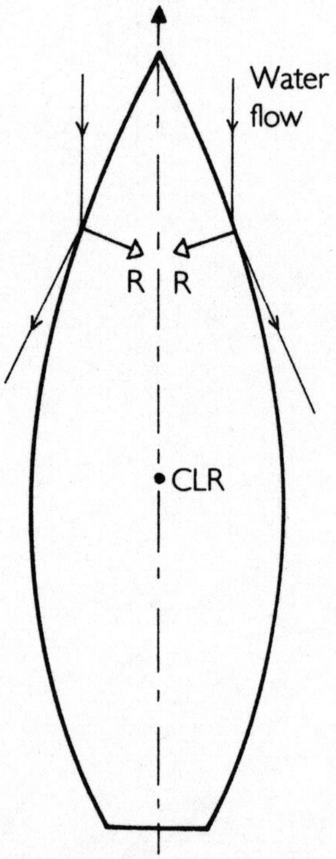

Boat heeled.

Water
flow

• CLR

Water
flow

• CLR

The resultants, R, due to the flow
of water past her bottom, are
equal and opposite:
trajectory along fore-and-aft
axis.

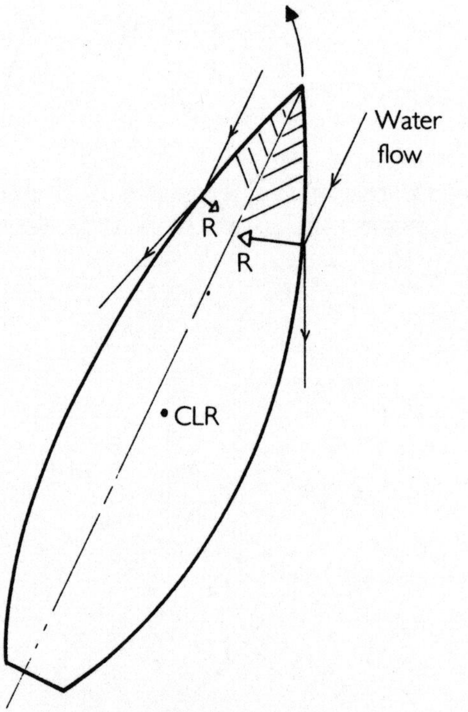

The resultants are unequal,
due to difference in
underwater surfaces in relation
to the plane of symmetry;
trajectory is a curve.

*Note*
Replacing a small jib with a bigger one should give **lee helm,**
but the more pronounced list may give her **weather helm**
instead.

# —Heaving-To—

## Purpose

To bring boat to a standstill:
    To rest crew (in heavy weather)
    For a meal
    To pick up man overboard
    To retrieve something that has carried away
    Having sprung a leak.
    etc.

**The operation** of heaving-to
As a general rule you will have
mainsail and a foresail up.

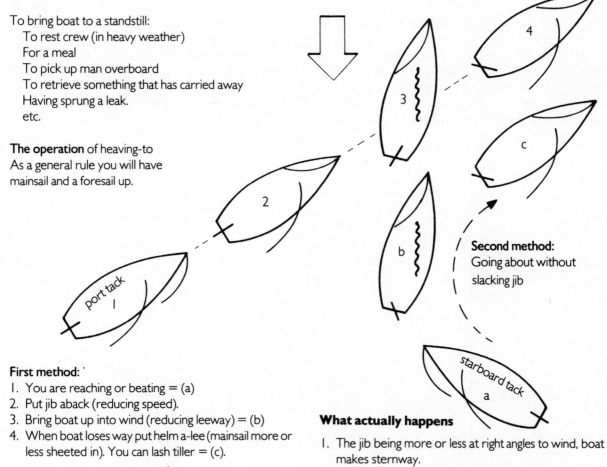

**Second method:**
Going about without
slacking jib

## First method:

1. You are reaching or beating = (a)
2. Put jib aback (reducing speed).
3. Bring boat up into wind (reducing leeway) = (b)
4. When boat loses way put helm a-lee (mainsail more or less sheeted in). You can lash tiller = (c).

## What actually happens

1. The jib being more or less at right angles to wind, boat makes sternway.
2. The mainsail, being sheeted in, then pushes the boat ahead.
3. But the helm, a-lee, luffs her up into the wind and stops her again.
4. Stage 2 is now repeated; and so on.

The result is a drift down-wind and forward.

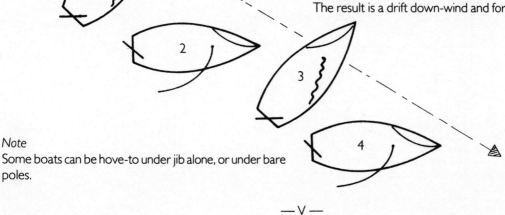

*Note*
Some boats can be hove-to under jib alone, or under bare poles.

## The 'Twelfths' Rule

The rise and fall of the tide between H.W. and L.W. is not at a constant rate and may, for some ports, be very irregular. The *Admiralty Tide Tables* include graphs for Standard Ports and rules for their application to Secondary Ports. However the rise and fall is fairly regular on British coasts, except in and near the Solent, and the height of tide at any time can be estimated by the simple 'Twelfths' rule:

Rise (or fall) in the 1st hour = 1/12 of Range
Rise (or fall) in the 2nd hour = 2/12 of Range
Rise (or fall) in the 3rd hour = 3/12 of Range
Rise (or fall) in the 4th hour = 3/12 of Range
Rise (or fall) in the 5th hour = 2/12 of Range
Rise (or fall) in the 6th hour = 1/12 of Range

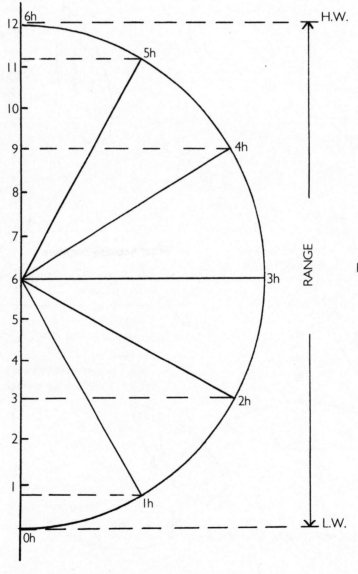

Remember: 1.2.3 – 3.2.1

# ──Summing Up──

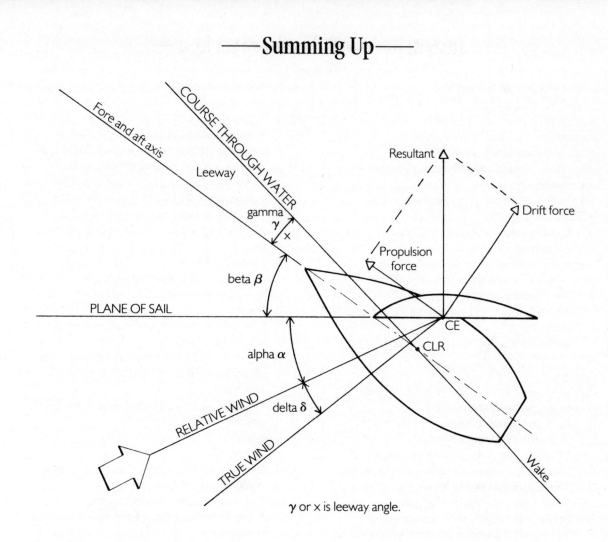

$\gamma$ or x is leeway angle.

For sail to fill $\alpha$ must be not less than 10° or 15°.

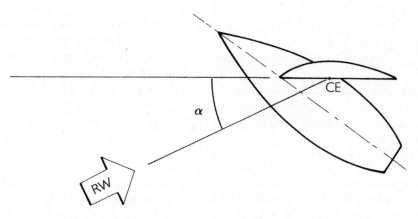

If $\alpha$ is more than 20°–25°, air flow becomes turbulent, (boat stalls).

—×—

# —— Instructions for the Shipwrecked ——

by Alain Bombard

(From *Naufragé volontaire*, Paris, Editions Arthaud)

I. Get into the life-raft.
   a) Verify the inflation pressure.
   b) Dry out the bottom with a bailer and then with a sponge.
   c) Make sure that it is airtight and watertight.
   d) Lash rafts together.
   e) 1. If the water is cold put up the canopy. Keep close together, do not ever bathe.
      2. If the water is warm put up the canopy. Relax, never expose yourself to the sun, wear a hat and sun glasses.
   f) Concentrate on your crew and think well ahead.
   g) Begin fishing, Keep calm and help the others to do so.

II. Signals
   a) Radio distress signals. Put up the aerial and try to establish communication. At 15 and 45 minutes past each hour try to transmit the MAYDAY signal.
   b) A looking glass. From now on try using it as a heliograph; it may be useful if an aircraft passes overhead or if a ship heaves in sight.
   c) Flares    See what you have got with you
   d) Smoke    and keep them ready for use.
   e) Fluorescine: put some overboard, but only by day and with a calm sea.

III. Food and water
   A. Water
   1. If you have a supply of fresh water:
      a) Ration it from the start: one litre per person per day is enough.
      b) Conserve your supply with the greatest care.
      c) If it rains, wash the canopy before you collect the fresh water. Taste it before you fill up.

   2. If you have no fresh water:
      a) Drink a little sea water, in small doses every hour, totalling not more than one litre per day.
      b) When you catch a fish make V shaped gashes in the skin of the back and drink the juices; one mouthful every half hour will be sufficient.
   3. Always drink slowly without swallowing too fast.
   4. Rest.
   5. Never drink urine.
   6. Blue sea-ice (old ice) is drinkable, the taste will tell you if it is fresh water.
   B. Food
   1. Fish: Off shore all fish are edible, even trigger-fish; eat the flesh raw.
   2. Plancton: put a sieve in the water (a shirt or the sea anchor) eat one or two spoonfuls a day (anti-scorbutic).
   3. Tinned food: only open one tin at a time and practise a strict economy.

IV. Dangers:
   A. Illness
   1. Seasickness: Avoid dehydration through lack of food; take anti-seasick pills.
   2. Constipation: Don't worry about it.
   3. Panic: Remember that it is contagious, but so is coolness.
   B. Sharks
   Do not throw rubbish overboard unless it is wrapped up.
   Do not take a dip unless somebody is on watch.
   Use anti-shark powder when you see a shark.
   **You can survive: others have done so before you** and remember that you can drink sea water for six days, fresh water three, sea water for six, fresh for three, and so on, indefinitely.
   Your life is at stake.

# Index